"After moving to LA I quickly discovered that Grand Central Market was the ultimate culinary paradise. It's the grand Mecca of inspiration for an aspiring chef like myself, which is why I'm super excited to add this cookbook to my collection." —JESSE TYLER FERGUSON

GRAND CENTRAL MARKET

has been bringing together the many traditions and flavors of Los Angeles since 1917. Its thirty-four stalls are filled with a mix of legacy tenants, representing the city's historic immigrant communities, and new vendors inspired by the city's cultural diversity. You might call it a melting pot, but it's more of a culinary quilt.

Now for the first time, GCM's cookbook shares the secrets of its vendors' culinary creativity. From Horse Thief BBQ's Nashville-style Hot Chicken Sando to Madcapra's Sumac-Beet Soda to Sarita's Spinach & Cheese Pupusas with Curtido, here are eighty-five recipes to make at home, plus spectacular photography that captures the food, the people, and the daily bustle and buzz in the aisles. Behind-the-scenes stories from GCM's dynamic history and interviews with popular vendors and lifelong visitors complete this insider's tour of LA's most vibrant gathering place.

Whether you've visited and want to re-create your favorite dishes at home or you're simply looking for a blast of authentic multicultural cuisine, *The Grand Central Market Cookbook* will take you to the progressive edge of today's new California cooking.

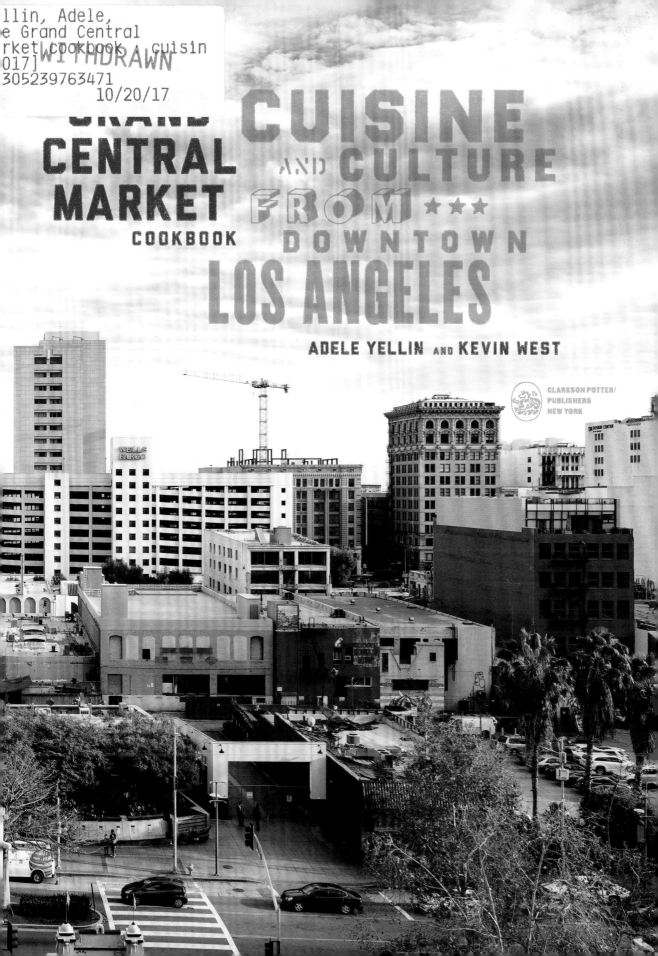

GRAND
CENTRAL
MARKET
COOKBOOK

CUISINE
AND CULTURE
FROM ***
DOWNTOWN
LOS ANGELES

ADELE YELLIN AND KEVIN WEST

CLARKSON POTTER/
PUBLISHERS
NEW YORK

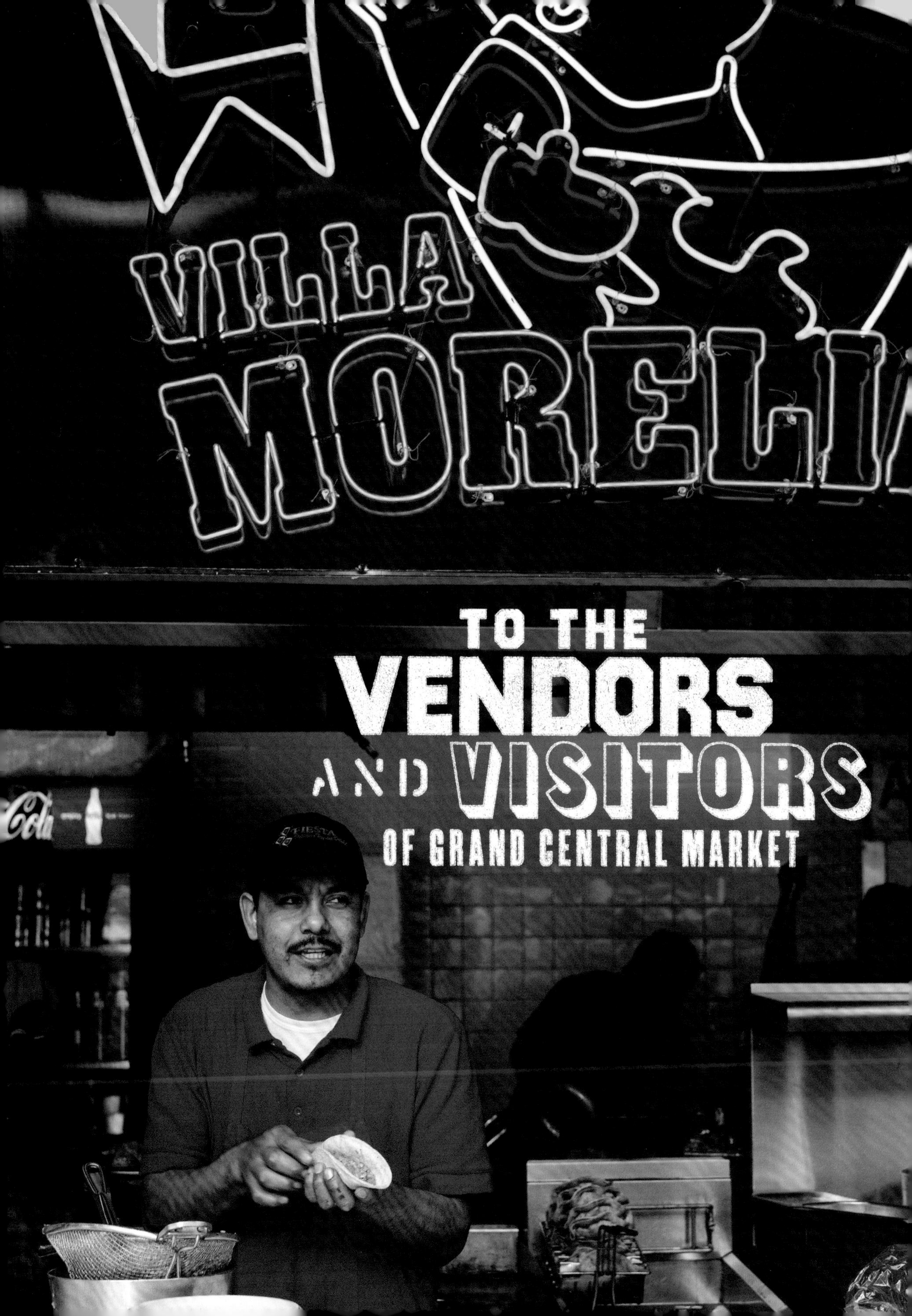

TO THE
VENDORS
AND VISITORS
OF GRAND CENTRAL MARKET

THE
PEOPLE
OF
GRAND CENTRAL
MARKET

From food, community.

If you drop by Eggslut late on a Sunday morning, you will find a long, sleepy line of breakfasters running through Grand Central Market, curling around the diner counter, edging past the Mexican seafood concession and eventually running into the crowd waiting for a crack at the lox and pastrami emerging from the smokers at Wexler's Deli. The macadamia-milk lattes at G&B are good enough to make coffee people babble in tongues. Belcampo serves what is arguably the best hamburger in town, sourced from the meat they raise themselves in the shadow of Mt. Shasta (which you can buy in the adjacent butcher shop). The fish stew assembled in the steam kettles at Mark Peel's Bombo reminds you why his Campanile was considered one of Americas great restaurants for so many years, and the chef is usually there to assemble it for you himself. Lydia Clarke of DTLA Cheese is the cheesemonger equivalent of a primo indie record store clerk. Madcapra serves its stunning if unconventional falafel with its own hand-fermented zhug. The warm, crusty baguettes from the Clark Street cart are superb. In the last couple of years, Grand Central Market has transformed itself from a tired, half-empty collection of food stalls into an essential food center that should be on the agenda of every visitor to LA. Owner Adele Yellin has managed to renovate the old market, a downtown fixture since 1917, without losing the splendid carnitas from Villa Moreliana, the dried chiles at Valeria's or the gorditas from Roast to Go. There has been controversy. But people on both sides of the gentrification debate seem to agree on the necessity of an Eggslut egg and cheese.

—Reprinted from **JONATHAN GOLD'S**
101 Best Restaurants, *Los Angeles Times*, November 4, 2015

"WHAT'S GOING ON HERE IS NOT JUST ABOUT GRAND CENTRAL MARKET. IT'S **LOS ANGELES** HISTORY. TACOS, RAMEN, DELI, COFFEE, FALAFEL— IT'S WHAT MAKES UP LA."

—MICHAEL KASSAR,
cofounder with Micah
Wexler of Wexler's Deli

I CAME TO LA FOR
OPPORTUNITY
AND THE SUNSHINE OF THE CITY. WHEN I OPENED HERE IN 2008, I DIDN'T THINK THE MARKET WOULD EVER BE LIKE IT IS TODAY. LIKE THE CITY, THE MARKET IS ALWAYS CHANGING, AND IT'S ALL FOR THE GOOD."
—FERNANDO VILLAGOMEZ,
owner of Villa Moreliana and La Tostadería

INTRO

GRAND CENTRAL MARKET IS A HISTORIC FOOD HALL IN DOWNTOWN LOS ANGELES.

It opened in 1917 at the corner of Broadway and Third Street and has been in continuous operation since. The floors of its hundred-and-fifteen-foot-wide open-air arcade are cement, the signs are neon, and a buzz hangs in the air. Its thirty-eight food stalls represent a mix of legacy tenants, drawn from LA's historic immigrant communities, and new vendors inspired by the kind of chef-driven/organic-local-seasonal/sustainable/humanely raised/vegetable-based/socially conscious/multicultural/mindful priorities that excite conscientious eaters today. Visitors sometimes call Grand Central Market a melting pot, but it's more of a culinary crazy quilt—differences don't melt together. Instead, one stall pops in contrast to what's alongside.

If you want to see how Los Angeles eats, this is the place to start. GCM offers breakfast, lunch, and dinner 361 days a year. The Hill Street entrance opens at 7 a.m. for G&B Coffee, and the rest of the Market comes to life an hour later, when a security guard rings the opening bell. At 9:50 p.m., the bell rings again to signal the Market will close in ten minutes. The aisles bustle with people all week.

On weekdays, office workers head down from Bunker Hill for lunch, and government employees walk over from nearby federal buildings. Jurors, easy to spot with their red badges, hurry in from the courthouse. Some of the same crowd comes back at happy hour, when they're joined by downtown residents and diners dropped off by Uber. But nothing beats a sunny weekend to bring out Angelenos of all stripes. At full tilt, GCM looks like Los Angeles—all of it. *GQ* called Grand Central Market "the most socially and economically integrated public space in America," and a single afternoon of people-watching proves it.

You see *bubbies, abuelas,* and *nainais;* families speaking English, Spanish, Korean, Japanese, Armenian, and Mandarin; packs of undergrads; couples of every age, color, and gender identity; Boyle Heights skate rats and fancy Westside ladies; health nuts and the hangover crowd. Tourists move through the crowd a little differently—more hesitant, perhaps overwhelmed by the choices and the luminous hodgepodge. They stop for selfies, look at press clippings, check their online guides, or follow in herds behind a flag-toting guide.

Everyone who goes to GCM is there to eat, but it's also a place to see LA from the inside out—a rare public venue where Angelenos climb out of their cars and literally rub shoulders. A trip to Grand Central Market is about more than just food. It's an *experience.* But it hasn't always been this way . . .

THE
HISTORY
OF GRAND CENTRAL MARKET
1917~1984
★

To really understand the Market's place in Los Angeles today, you have to rewind a century. Los Angeles was a young city then. It was before the tech boom, before the aerospace boom, before the postwar real estate boom. Architectural modernism had not yet created the clean lines and indoor-outdoor lifestyle of the SoCal good life. Hollywood had barely begun to emerge as a global dream factory.

Back then, Los Angeles was booming because of oil, oranges, and water. The underground petroleum that seeped to the surface at the La Brea tar pits also spewed gushers of dollars into the California economy. The citrus industry, which had literally taken root in Riverside in the 1890s, was by now shipping hundreds of thousands of trainloads of golden fruit to the East Coast, thanks to the novelty of refrigeration. And a brilliant engineer named William Mulholland had just opened the Los Angeles aqueduct to carry water from the foot of the Sierra Nevada mountains to the thirsty acreage around a former ranching town once known as La Ciudad de Nuestra Señora de Los Angeles. (If the story rings a bell, that's because it was the inspiration for the 1974 movie *Chinatown*.)

The beginning of the twentieth century was also the golden age of LA's Broadway, a central thoroughfare for pedestrians, streetcars, and automobiles alike. Stores lined the way, with doctors' and lawyers' offices upstairs. The wide avenue was dotted with elegant theaters, some of which are still standing. You could almost say that in 1917, Broadway *was* downtown Los Angeles. Nearby Bunker Hill was then covered with stately Victorian mansions and a lavish resort hotel shaded by palm trees. From the top, where Frank Gehry's Disney Hall today perches like a titanium crown, you could see across the Los Angeles Basin to the Pacific Ocean in one direction and the snow-capped San Gabriel Mountains in the other. The neighborhood's stylish residents rode up to and down from

GLORIA DIAZ (pictured, opposite) has been coming to GCM for as long as she can remember—memories that stretch back to the 1940s. "I have retired and I figure, why should I be cooking?" says Gloria, "so I come here instead." Gloria lives across the street in a senior housing complex at the foot of Bunker Hill. She stood at the front of the line on Knead's opening day, and made a point of dropping by the 2016 GCM Holidays marketplace to check out the tamale pop-up and talk to the staff about the status of Angels Flight. (The short funicular railroad that runs up and down Bunker Hill had been closed for repairs and Gloria was eager to see it running again.) Gloria keeps a busy schedule, but one morning she dropped by G&B to have a decaf latte and reminisce about what has changed at GCM over the decades—and what hasn't.

GCM: When did you first come to the Market?

DIAZ: When I was a child. I was about seven or eight years old on the first visit I remember. My grandmother had a house in Watts, so we'd come here on the Red Line—that was the trolley car. Whatever my mother needed for groceries, she'd buy here and we'd spend the day. Everybody knew each other, and we liked all the vendors. They were very kind.

GCM: When was that?

DIAZ: I was born in '32, so it was in the forties. My mother was from Mexico and my dad was from Watts. I was born in Chinatown at the French hospital, delivered by a German doctor. So I rest my case: That's why I love everyone.

GCM: Where did you live then?

DIAZ: We lived on Bunker Hill. It was all old Victorian homes, like San Francisco. Little by little, the rich people left, and the big houses were made into apartments. It was a community up there. You probably can't believe it, because of the way it looks now. [Today Bunker Hill is topped with office towers.] Now that I'm in my senior days, I'm on Bunker Hill again. I was destined to come back.

GCM: When you were a child, did you take Angels Flight?

DIAZ: [An amused look.] We lived on Angels Flight! Two rides for a nickel. We kids used to ride it all day. We had a ball. I miss it. It's part of the history of this place.

GCM: How was the Market different back then?

DIAZ: Oh my gosh! It was cheap! Of course, looking back on those times, everything seems cheap compared to today.

GCM: Was it the same mix of vendors?

DIAZ: There were more grocers. It was a great big market. But people would also come here to eat. There was a Chinese restaurant, and I think there have always been tacos.

GCM: Who are your favorite vendors today?

DIAZ: There are so many. I like the breakfast at Jose Chiquito. Then there's the barbeque place [Horse Thief]. And I like China Cafe—us Latins like Chinese food, the noodles and the pork—and the Italian place, Knead. I love their cannoli; I buy two to take home.

GCM: Some people have complained about the changes that have happened in recent years.

DIAZ: I know. I've heard that, too. But you have to go through change. That's life, you know?

GCM: The city has changed, too.

DIAZ: And it's still going to be changing. But the people are the same. They are still very kind to me. I've gotten to know everybody practically. We talk. Even now that I'm a senior, I still meet people here all the time. It's just like before—everybody knows each other.

Bunker Hill aboard Angels Flight, a short funicular railroad that was the city's first public transportation system. Its terminus was a few steps away from where Grand Central Public Market opened to the hungry public in 1917.

When the Homer Laughlin family opened the market that year, there were no supermarkets as we know them today. People went to neighborhood shops— the corner grocer, the greengrocer, the baker, the butcher. Big cities such as Los Angeles, New York, Philadelphia, Detroit, and Atlanta also offered their citizens the amenity of "public markets," which brought the greengrocer, the baker, and the butcher together under one roof. Public markets became a destination by uniting a city's worth of independent vendors in a single arcade.

Grand Central Public Market was true to its name—*grand*. It covered some 80,000 square feet, with two levels of retail space and a subterranean network of hallways lined with storage rooms, walk-in freezers, and refrigerators large enough to park a Model A Ford. Dumbwaiters from the basement to the street-level sales floor allowed vendors to stock their stalls without ever having to venture into the crowded aisles. It was a modern marvel.

The Market fed a million people (or so said a 1922 advertising brochure) with over ninety stalls that included fruit vendors, bakeries, butchers, and delis. Hot lunches were also sold "to save time and effort for the Market patrons, but also to make their [downtown] shopping tours pleasant," according to the brochure. It described twenty fruit and vegetable vendors; fourteen butchers, "all equipped with sanitary refrigerated cases"; multiple bakers and confectioners; soda fountains; a coffee roaster; fishmongers; and dry goods merchants. There were two florists—Suenaga and Suzuki—and two bacon sellers. Cheese and dairy filled several stalls. A grain mill sold fresh flour. One stall offered nothing but eggs, stacked in trays by the hundred dozen. Mr. Pagano, who called himself "The Celery Heart Man," staked his entire business on one product: "We were instrumental in introducing celery hearts to Los Angeles housewives, and we would like to interest you," read his ad. A vendor named May's rented multiple stalls to sell mayonnaise, olives, pickles, and sauerkraut. XYZ Fruit Co. boasted, "Our displays of fruits and vegetables are so temptingly arranged that you will seem to want everything that we sell."

Dinettes, cafeterias, and coffee shops sold prepared food. The Dinner Pail offered carryout, and a Chinese restaurant in the basement reflected the city's already established ethnic diversity. Multiple delicatessens were a reminder that east of downtown, Boyle Heights was then predominantly Jewish. Other immigrant communities from Eastern Europe had settled at the north end of Broadway, in the area that is today's Historic Chinatown.

After the crash of 1929, the Market rebounded and entered its second heyday in the 1940s. Historian Kevin Starr's book *The Dream Endures: California Enters the 1940s* describes it as a defining landmark for the entire city. (See page 20 for GCM customer Gloria Diaz's memories of the Market in the 1940s.) Near the end of the decade, a man named Beach Lyon became the manager of GCM and eventually bought it from the Laughlin family. During Lyon's years, which spanned the economic golden age of the postwar boom and stretched into the 1980s, GCM evolved to reflect the growing diversity of Los Angeles. Irish, Jewish, and Asian

immigrants, among others, sold goods to the increasingly multiethnic population shopping at the Market.

Pictures from the 1940s show sleek steel-and-glass service counters and confident, prosperous shoppers; it was a time when ladies still wore white gloves to shop and men strolled out in hats. Skip forward to the '70s, and men started to stroll out in bell bottoms. The Market still endured as a shopping destination. For politicians seeking city or state office, an election-eve appearance at Grand Central was mandatory. (Current mayor, Eric Garcetti, pictured above, continues the tradition.)

What you can't see in the pictures from those days was that beyond the Market's walls, downtown had lost much of its luster. The construction of the freeways two decades earlier had caused the suburbs to boom. The streetcar that had once moved shoppers through the area was gone—and so was the dynamism of Broadway. Prosperity had long since abandoned Bunker Hill for neighborhoods farther west—Hancock Park,

Shopping Tips

SHOPPING EFFICIENCY

Through aisles of food products you may pass from Broadway to Hill Street. Every possible entrance and exit advantage has been utilized.

250 feet Display Cases

IRA YELLIN WAS FIRST INTRODUCED TO GCM AS A CHILD.

His family moved to LA in the 1940s and went there on Sundays to stock up on weekly groceries. Ira always remembered it as a busy place with unfamiliar sights and smells and interesting people whom he loved to watch, even if he could not eat the magnificent hams on display (the family kept kosher). That memory lasted a lifetime and certainly compelled his decision to acquire the Market in 1984.

Adele was no stranger to GCM, either. An avid cook, she was always trying new recipes. In the 1960s she started making a dish that required poblano chiles, and, at the time, GCM was the only place in town to buy them. She had been doing her specialty shopping at the Market long before Ira made it part of the Yellin family.

As Ira and Adele built a life and a family together, the Market was always part of it.

Their daughter, Jessica, recalls that when she was ten years old, she felt proud that all the vendors knew her father and stopped him to say hello. The Market's display cases—taller than she was— held a world of curiosities. At the spice vendor, Adele explained that the many boxes of red powder were different kinds of ground chiles, and each box held a different flavor powder. Ira showed Jessica the pig's snouts and pig's feet on display at the butcher counter and taught her that some cuisines considered them delicacies. Jessica especially loved the candy stand that sold lollipops bigger than her head.

Seth also remembers when he was about ten walking through the Market with his father. The unfamiliar ingredients fascinated him: mounds of pepitas, baskets of mole negro and mole verde, garlands of dried chile peppers, piles of chicharron and carne asada. He watched a machine at Homeboy Tortillas crank out fresh tortillas by the dozen. At Roast to Go, he peered through the steamy counter and asked his dad what tacos de cabeza were. Ira replied they were made from lamb's head and invited him to try one. Seth chose carnitas instead and relived that moment in the summer of 2015 when he took his son, Isaiah, then age four, to GCM for his first taste of real carnitas.

"I couldn't help but think," recalls Seth, "that my experience with Isaiah has been lived by so many families over the last century trying food both familiar and foreign, but all of it perfectly Angeleno."

Beverly Hills—while other downtown or downtown-adjacent neighborhoods had started to drain in the 1950s, part of a nationwide demographic trend that saw middle-class residents leave city centers for the suburban ideal of a backyard with a barbecue and a pool. The same story played out in New York, Chicago, Detroit, Atlanta, Nashville—many of the same cities that had once supported vibrant public markets. LA's white flight was exacerbated by the Watts riots of 1965. As the urban core emptied, rents dropped and storefronts shuttered.

But other LA residents saw opportunity downtown. A wave of new Latino and Asian immigrants moved in and opened businesses. They brought the foods and flavors of their homelands, making Grand Central Market a place for specialty ingredients and value prices. Over time, the multiple delis and butchers of the 1920s gave way to multiple taquerias, a carniceria, a tortilleria, and steam-table Chinese food.

1984–2012: Ira's Vision

That's more or less where things stood in the 1980s, when Ira Yellin looked at downtown and saw not a faded past but a vibrant future. Ira was a Harvard-educated lawyer who had developed his interest in urbanism and urban renewal while getting his master's degree in law from the University of California, Berkeley. Once he became a lawyer and real estate developer, he kept his eye on the property, even though vendors who retired were slow to be replaced and the surrounding neighborhood—what is now called the Historic Core—had deteriorated.

But Ira believed. He understood that the Market remained vital, thanks to Latino and Asian shoppers who came in for affordable meats and produce, tacos and burgers, and Sunday outings with their families. He felt that downtown could be brought back to life—could be restored to the downtown he had loved growing up (see page 23)—if developers renovated the beautiful historic buildings sitting vacant. He believed that residents of LA yearned for a place where they could mingle with people from all walks of life. The city of cars and suburbs has always lacked public spaces to create community in that way. Ira recognized GCM as an exception—a democratic place to gather. He believed the Market had a future because he believed downtown would eventually bounce back, and he wanted to lead that revival. Many of Ira's friends thought he was crazy.

He brought together investors, the Community Redevelopment Agency, and the Metropolitan Transit Authority in a public-private partnership to buy a group of historic buildings—GCM, the Million Dollar Theatre, and the Bradbury Building. The partnership invested millions in GCM for seismic upgrades, new wiring and plumbing, and a parking garage—the baseline modernization to bring an old place up to code. Ira also modernized the name to Grand Central Market.

But Ira was ahead of his time. When he died prematurely in 2002 of lung cancer, never having been a smoker, downtown Los Angeles was not yet the vibrant urban center he had imagined; the changes he foresaw wouldn't arrive for another decade. He left his stake in the Market partnership to his wife, Adele, and for years she entrusted the day-to-day operations to Anne Peaks, vice president of operations, and long-time manager Filomena Eriman, who retired in 2013 after forty years. Adele didn't make changes, because she never quite believed Ira was gone. Still in mourning, she felt like she was just waiting until he returned to take charge again.

The Market drifted along until the 2008 financial crisis. Stall after stall closed, until the vacancy rate topped 40 percent. Other vendors stayed in place only because Adele forgave their unpaid rent for months—sometimes for years. Most observers sensed doom.

2012–Present: Adele's Vision

Around 2012, after years of the Market's languishing, Adele noticed "green shoots" of economic activity beginning to appear downtown (to use President Obama's term of cautious optimism). Chef Josef Centeno opened his restaurant Bäco Mercat; it eventually spawned four more Centeno-owned restaurants within a block. A string of downtown bars from Cedd Moses, including the Golden Golpher and a neo-speakeasy called the Varnish, helped introduce LA to "to the new cocktailians," a phrase coined by Pulitzer Prize–winning food critic Jonathan Gold, a longtime fan of GCM. Chef Ari Taymor opened his experimental kitchen Alma on South Broadway, and it was named America's Best New Restaurant by *Bon Appétit* in 2013. Downtown's Business Improvement District released a report showing that the residential population had quietly swelled to fifty thousand. Many were young professionals living in loft conversions. They all needed places to eat and drink. In retrospect, it's clear that downtown was on the verge of becoming a hot "new" neighborhood.

With a renewed hopefulness, Adele took the reins and started putting together a team to help her revitalize the Market. Looking back, the only reason her consortium of investors let her hire such a motley crew was because they believed the Market was already a lost cause. They didn't believe that Adele, the glamorous widow, could revive the Market without Ira in charge. Adele, by the way, is tiny in stature and wears the chic, dark-palette designer clothes of an art collector, but she also buzzes with energy and speaks with the big voice of an old-school dame. An art deco gold serpent watch always twists around her tanned wrist. Adele is a pistol, and the doubters underestimated her.

Adele first brought in the development firm RM|d to help her devise a new business plan; soon Matt Nolan, a twenty-nine-year-old financial strategist with matinee-idol looks and

a math-nerd personality, had a permanent desk in the Market office. For her new business director—the person to execute the plan Matt created—Adele turned to Christophe Farber, a former screenwriter who had attended college with her son. Through her daughter-in-law, Jenny Comita, Adele then met Joseph Shuldiner and Kevin West of Headspace Consulting and hired them as creative directors to advise on a new mission statement, rebranding, website redesign, and—most important—outreach to potential new tenants.

Adele convened the team and recounted the history of the Market, explaining what Ira had done in his day. She acknowledged that vendors were not doing well, but she believed that many of the legacy tenants had the talent and tenacity to rebound if she could just shore up the Market's customer base—she was committed to keeping tenants, not getting rid of them. "The real estate guys all say kick everyone out and close the place down," she said with frustration. She paused a second. "Fuck 'em. They're a bunch of men in suits who think I can't do this because I'm the widow. I'm not going to do it their way. I'll do it *my* way. And if I fail—oh, well. At least I tried."

The question then was how to attract the young professionals who had moved downtown and didn't even know about the Market. She had to bring in fresh concepts that would appeal to the new downtown. She'd already hired and fired some fancy restaurant consultant who hadn't been able to see her vision. He'd suggested chain restaurants. Adele rolled her eyes, as if to say, How could anyone mistake *me* for a chain restaurant kind of gal? The idea of leasing GCM to a single large tenant was even worse. She wanted local start-ups, not national corporations.

Adele said firmly, "This place is for everybody. I don't want it turned into a Whole Foods. When it opened, it was called Grand Central *Public* Market. That's what I want. It's a place for the people." She imagined a culinary village filled with independent businesses and entrepreneurs. She wanted quality but not snobbery. She didn't want to duplicate San Francisco's Ferry Building Marketplace—"it's great for San Francisco, but this is LA"—and she considered GCM's history a unique asset not shared by newly built food halls like New York's Chelsea Market. Her direction for the future would be defined by the Market's past.

When the last member of the core team signed on—Jim Yeager, president of the PR firm breakwhitelight—everyone sat down in a room to place words around Adele's vision. What emerged from that day's brainstorm was a mission statement for the new GCM website:

> Grand Central Market's mission is to celebrate the cuisines and cultures of Los Angeles. Our commitment is to preserve the legacy of a historic downtown landmark, to gather the city's many communities around a shared table, and to nurture the next generation of local businesses.

Chris boiled it all down to a three-word motto:

> From food, community.

Jim tossed out a marketing tagline:

> Amazing Food. Amazing Place.

And the Market revitalization was under way.

SO WHY *DID* IRA YELLIN BUY GRAND CENTRAL MARKET?

He answered the question himself in a 1989 profile by *Angeles* magazine titled "Bright Guy, Big City."

"I like cities. I love an urban context . . . I mean, I hate suburbs . . . Where are the guts of a city? Whenever I went downtown I was always trying to gravitate to it, to find the core—and I'd always wind up in Grand Central Market. I loved the mix of people there, and I always think that when you have human energy like that there should also be a way to translate that energy into a valid economic investment. I went to the Market day after day for a period of weeks, and I looked out at one side and saw all these skyscrapers looming up above me, just a block away on Bunker Hill. [At the Market's other entrance Yellin saw] this bustling Hispanic secret of Broadway. And it was like two worlds colliding . . . So I said to myself . . . *this area has got to be a good area.*

"Almost everybody had overlooked the historic part of the city. I know that the time is going to come, very shortly, when they're all going to be moving in this direction. But that's what I saw. I saw an opportunity."

THE
VENDORS

★

Adele's grand plan to revitalize the market was to bring in the most exciting young chefs to join the iconic legacy eateries for a singular dining experience in one of Los Angeles's most historic neighborhoods. She and her small team sought out hot food-truck operators and young chefs looking for a first foothold—a place to incubate new ideas. Adele's sales pitch boiled down to hope and trust. "We're willing to take a risk on you," she told potential vendors, "if you'll take a risk on us."

Many of the chefs and entrepreneurs GCM initially brought in were underground heroes but barely known to the public at large. G&B Coffee had just launched out of a literal storage closet at Sqirl, the newly opened and now famous café from Jessica Koslow. While Chris and Matt, the business guys, negotiated lease terms with G&B, the Market's very first new vendor was already set to start serving.

Sticky Rice opened on April 30, 2013, with a colorful (and noisy) blessing by Buddhist monks (see page 185 for that story). Joseph and Kevin had met Sticky Rice's owner, David Tewasart, at the Altadena Farmers Market, where his stall had won a loyal following for its home-style Thai cooking made with organic ingredients. David wanted to serve authentic Thai street food the way it was served in Thailand—hot! But because he was unsure of the Market's future, he didn't want a long-term lease in case the project didn't fly. He agreed to a one-year pop-up in an empty stall with a four-top burner and a grill left behind when the previous tenant, a burger joint, closed in the aftermath of 2008. Within weeks, the editorial staff from the *LA Times* food section were regulars at the Sticky Rice counter.

Civilian customers began to arrive as well. In those early days, the lunch crowd at the Market was so sparse that the two young men in business suits stood out as they made a beeline through the center of the Market toward Sticky Rice one day. The tall one looked eager; the shorter one, perplexed. They stopped in front of the Sticky Rice stall, and Tall gave his colleague a spot-on description of the menu, clearly having visited before. You could see the thrill in his face as he shared this cool thing he'd discovered. Shorty nodded his approval, and they sat down at the counter to eat. Moments like that made it clear that Adele's vision would save the Market. Excitement is infectious, especially when it comes to food, and GCM now had word of mouth on its side.

A year later, David signed a long-term lease and remodeled his stall; since then he's expanded with a second stall, Sticky Rice II, serving Thai noodles.

That same summer, Kevin heard rumors about a food truck with a devilish name that served divine egg sandwiches. He followed Eggslut's Twitter feed to a street corner downtown, where chef Alvin Cailan stuck out

MICHAEL PALMER—CO-OWNER WITH HIS WIFE, EVA EIN, of McConnell's Fine Ice Creams, which opened its GCM location in 2014—has been coming to GCM his entire life, ever since he was a kid growing up in nearby Hancock Park. He recalls visiting the Market with his grandfather in the early 1980s:

"The men in my family all worked in downtown Los Angeles, on the sixteenth floor of one of the concrete-glass-and-steel towers that cluster to the west of the Historic Core. Downtown was so strangely inconsistent in scale—in vibe—with the suburban sprawl that decades ago hijacked the rest of Los Angeles, as if those towers were daring anyone to suggest that LA was anything less than *a real city*.

"From his office on the corner of Sixth Street and Flower, my grandfather and I would head downhill to Grand Central Market for lunch. I remember the distinct smell of the place—huge pots of lard, cooked down and filled with all manner of pig parts—and concrete floors, covered with sawdust shavings and discolored from years of traffic and spilled *everything*.

"There was a lost-in-time feeling about the place, even then. Stepping into the Market, I had the sense of being somewhere else. The Market's cultural mix only heightened that feeling—Mexican and Chinese vendors, the spice counters, a strange apothecary counter. It may have been a bit scary, but it was magnificent. That I was with my grandfather made it safe. That it was all about food made it wonderful. Grand Central Market with all its flavors was a place to be transported, especially for a white kid from flavorless Hancock Park."

his head. Alvin came in for a tour of GCM during a grimy summer heat wave when the Market seemed abandoned, but he immediately understood Adele's vision and signed up for an empty stall facing the Broadway entrance. The trickle of adventurous eaters who arrived for Eggslut's October 2013 opening grew month by month into a flood of groupies—and the crowds haven't ebbed since.

The fresh clientele helped GCM's legacy vendors grow, too. Fernando Villagomez, owner of the carnitas stall Villa Moreliana from 2008, put himself through Le Cordon Bleu cooking school and opened a second business, La Tostadería, in 2015. Tacos Tumbras a Tomas from 1995 almost doubled its square footage, and China Cafe from 1959 started drawing up plans to revamp its cramped kitchen and iconic wraparound counter. Marlon Medina, a line cook who started at Jose Chiquito in 2007, saved up enough to buy the business in 2016 and has grown sales substantially with an upgraded menu.

For the Market, there was no looking back.

SUCCESS

Today it would be natural to describe the Market's revival as a culinary success story, or maybe to talk about it as a business story, a case study in scrappy American entrepreneurialism. Either telling would be wrong—or at least incomplete.

The success of the Market revitalization that began in 2012 boils down to three factors. First is Adele's insistence that the Market remain a public gathering place for all the cuisines and cultures of Los Angeles. Second, the creativity and hard work of GCM's vendors. Third and most important is that the public *wanted it* to succeed. Customers rallied around GCM as an emblem of downtown's resurgence and a focal point for civic pride. Grand Central Market survived because it caught the spirit of what was happening all around it in downtown.

And that is perhaps Adele's most personal measure of success. The Yellin name has been synonymous with urban renewal since Ira bought the Market in 1984, and Adele understood her first duty was to safeguard that family legacy. But her second duty, as she saw it, was to safeguard the public trust of Grand Central Market as a historic landmark shared by generations of Angelenos. Hers was a civic vision, not just a business plan.

Visitors who knew the place as children, as Ira did, express relief that it still exists. First-time visitors sometimes seem amazed to discover any landmark with so much history in a city that is generally neglectful of the past. A few critics, of course, have lamented what they see as the disruptive process of gentrification in downtown, but Adele saw no alternative for the future except fatal irrelevance. "People will criticize me if I change the Market," she said at the time. "And people will criticize me if I don't change the Market. I can't just let it die."

Cities survive and thrive because of change. It is obvious that Los Angeles is not the little town of big dreamers that was in 1917. Today it's a global metropolis integrated into a flat-world economy. The reality of Los Angeles as a twenty-first-century city is exciting precisely because it looks like the future of America, not its past. The same can be said of Grand Central Market. Is it the same as it was in 1917? Of course not. For one hundred years, the Market has reflected the city of Los Angeles, and it continues to do so. The Market's diversity of vendors and visitors reflects Los Angeles *today*. There are many reasons that matters. A big one is that the food at GCM represents a dynamic mash-up of cuisines and cultures from around the world. It is a place to discover the crazy quilt that is LA's food scene, a legacy of one hundred years of immigration and cultural diversity. Which is another way of saying the food at Grand Central Market today looks a lot like the future of American food tomorrow. It's a place where food becomes community.

"Years ago the only reason people went to downtown Los Angeles was to dump a body. But that's all changed. This is LA's Brooklyn now. The place is bustling with new reasons to go there. One of those new reasons is about a hundred years old. What I love about Grand Central Market is what I love about the other great markets in the world: It's a microcosm of life where many cultures and ethnicities and foods all come together. You can turn left and get a pork taco and turn to the right and get wonton soup. It's phenomenal."

—PHIL ROSENTHAL, *I'LL HAVE WHAT PHIL'S HAVING*

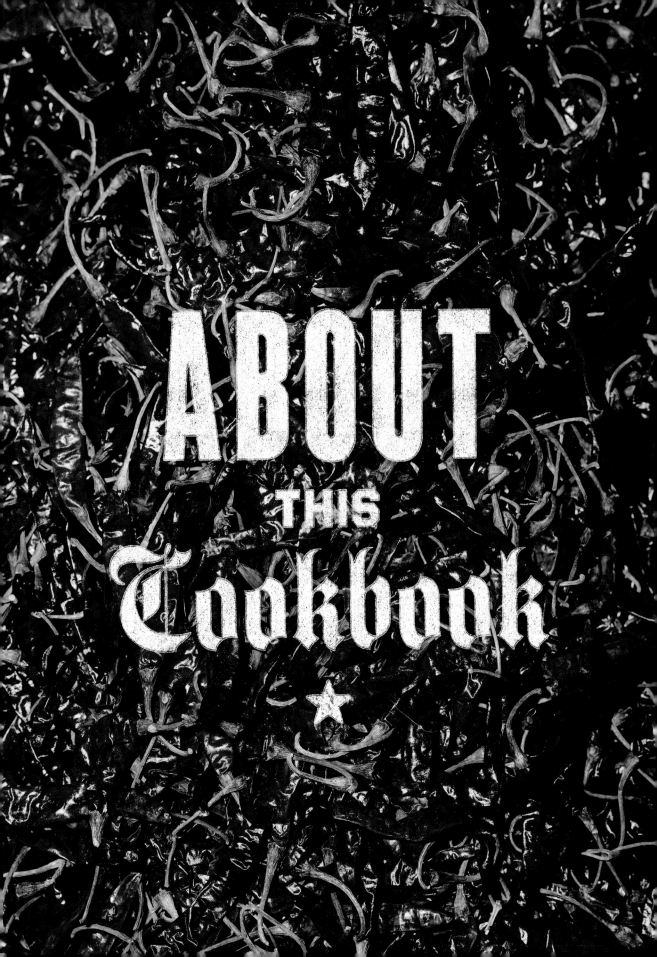

ABOUT THIS Cookbook

★

Every food vendor at Grand Central Market contributed to *The Grand Central Market Cookbook*. Their recipes were adapted—and in some cases, reimagined—to work in a home kitchen. A handful of "Market Recipes" were developed from scratch with inspiration from ingredients sold at the Market, such as the dried chiles from Valeria's and the mole pastes at Chiles Secos. As a recipe anthology, this cookbook is, in a way, like old-fashioned community cookbooks, popular in the '50s and '60s, in which each contributor shared a cherished recipe to create what we'd now call crowd-sourced content. But a key difference is that Grand Central Market represents not one community, but many. This is a *communities* cookbook. You'll have a lot to choose from—that's just part of the Grand Central Market experience.

Visitors to the Market respond to the culinary array in various ways. Some target a specific stall on each visit—paella from Prawn Sustainable Seafood today and pierogis from Golden Road Brewing next time. Other visitors mix and match, maybe starting with a half dozen oysters from The Oyster Gourmet, then grabbing some ceviche at La Tostadería or a lengua taco at Ana Maria. Couples might coordinate their plans: You get a sundae from McConnell's, I'll get cookies from Valerie Confections, and we'll share. Groups often split up to order, then convene at a table on the patio to compare: smoked brisket from Horse Thief BBQ, tofu al pastor from Ramen Hood, farro salad from DTLA Cheese, fresh fruit from District Market, some tomato salad from Madcapra, and fries from Belcampo Meat Company. Then everyone swaps—an edible tour of the Market—and makes up new combinations. Why not put some Sticky Rice papaya salad on that *pupusa* from Sarita's? Or add fries to a falafel sandwich? Slap some smoked salmon on a pizza? (All those inventions, by the way, are menu hacks proposed by Zach Brooks on Thrillist.com.)

Approach this cookbook in a similar way. There's a range of options in the pages ahead. You can dip in wherever you like; it's an invitation to mix and match. What kind of meal do you want to eat today? Which three or four recipes to you want to put together for a party? Do you want to make something fast and easy, or to create something memorable?

Navigation

The book is organized into seven thematic chapters: Breakfast; Tacos, Etc.; Carbs; Happy Hour; Meat and Fish; Veg; and Sweets. There are several ways to find recipes. If you're hungry for breakfast but don't know what you want, scan through the recipe list for the Breakfast chapter (page 40), where you can choose between huevos rancheros (from Jose Chiquito) or yeasted waffles (from G&B Coffee). Or if you know you want to make something from your favorite stall, go straight to the appendix on page 246, where recipes are grouped by vendor, and you'll find that Sarita's contributed recipes for *pupusas*, *curtido*, and *carne guisada*, while Knead & Co pasta chef Bruce Kalman offered up his giardiniere pickles and big meatballs in amatriciana sauce. And the usual index at the back of the book (page 250) lets you search for specific items by ingredient, whether it's chicken or kale.

To put it in very broad terms, *The Grand Central Market Cookbook* brings together three global culinary traditions: Anglo-European/Mediterranean, Latino, and Asian. Each of those large traditions could be subdivided into national cuisines (Latino = Mexican + Salvadoran + Peruvian) or even subnational categories (Mexican = Sinaloan seafood + Oaxacan mole + border-region tacos + SoCal burritos). But regional variations aside, it's safe to say that this cookbook embraces three distinctive global palates, which also means it draws on three distinctive global pantries. For example, if Mediterranean cooking requires olive oil, then it's also true that Latin cuisines use dried chiles and masa, and that Asian cuisines need soy sauce and ginger. But don't be scared off by that!

With very few exceptions, the ingredients you'll need to cook from this book are readily available in any supermarket that has even the smallest section of Asian and Latin specialty products. Once-exotic items like coconut milk, dried chiles, pepitas, and fish sauce are now widespread. Key fresh ingredients such as ginger, cilantro, and jalapeños are commonplace. Obviously, if you live in or near Los Angeles, Grand Central Market offers one-stop shopping. Online retailers including Amazon stock almost every ingredient you'll find in the pages ahead.

When a recipe calls for a specific item that might be difficult to source, such as mole *ajonjoli* or chayote, a more accessible alternative is given when possible. Only a few recipes are meant to showcase a signature specialty ingredient, such as *tunas*—prickly pear fruit (page 168). But even then, suggestions are given for how to adapt the recipe to use another, more commonly available fruit, such as pineapple.

A Note on Salt

The recipes ahead will specify either fine sea salt or kosher salt; different chefs have different preferences. The two are not interchangeable! A teaspoon of fine sea salt (or granulated table salt) can contain nearly twice

as much sodium as a teaspoon of Diamond Crystal kosher salt, because the fine grains pack together more densely than flaky kosher salt. That means sea salt is nearly twice as salty as the same amount of kosher salt.

Please note which kind of salt a recipe calls for, and consider the salt you have on hand. As with any recipe, use common sense if the salt level seems out of whack, and always adjust to taste.

A Note on Cooking Fats

The other most common ingredients in this cookbook fall under the general rubric of fats: oils, butter, and lard.

Several types of oil are specified. Olive oil always means extra-virgin, and it can't be replaced by another oil without affecting the recipe's result. Always use top-quality olive oil (avoid anything that says "pure" or "blended" on the label), and keep it fresh by storing it in a cool, dark place (the cabinet above the stove is the worst place).

Toasted sesame oil also has a specific flavor and use; it can't be swapped with anything else without changing the dish dramatically.

On the other hand, the neutral vegetable oils (safflower, canola, peanut, sunflower, corn, grapeseed, refined coconut) can be used interchangeably. If a recipe calls for "oil for frying," a neutral vegetable oil is the best choice.

Butter should always be unsalted.

When GCM opened one hundred years ago, lard was widely used in America, before the cottonseed oil industry's successful marketing campaigns turned consumers against it and converted them to hydrogenated oils such as Crisco, a manufacturing innovation. Many traditional cuisines never stopped using lard, and chefs in recent years have revived an interest in lard's superior cooking qualities. Most independent butcher shops sell lard for cooking and extra-fine leaf lard for baking. Both are well worth seeking out. For the recipes in this book, if lard is called for as the cooking fat (such as for sautéing), it can be replaced with vegetable oil.

EQUIPMENT

★

Most recipes in *The Grand Central Market Cookbook* can be made with the basic cooking equipment you have at home. Your standard knives, pots, pans, and mixing bowls will get you through.

A few recipes call for a specific tool—a box grater, a mandoline, a mortar and pestle, a blender or food processor—but otherwise the recipes have been adapted to avoid the specialized equipment found in professional kitchens.

There are just two exceptions: to make Press Brothers Juicery's signature juices from scratch (pages 68–70), you'll need a juicer. (They recommend Breville's Juice Fountain Cold with cold spin technology.) And the Pressed Cucumber Salad from Ramen Hood (page 204) calls for a vacuum sealer. Without it, you won't be able to get the translucent jade-like effect of pressed cucumbers, although you can still make and enjoy the dressing on any cucumbers, pressed or not.

TIMING

★

If a recipe requires notable advance planning—letting dough rest overnight or marinating meat for several hours, for example—that step will be called out in the recipe headnote. Multistep recipes might also suggest strategies for time management, perhaps to make the dipping sauce the day before cooking. Dishes such as *posole* (pork and hominy stew, page 191) actually improve overnight in the fridge.

A FINAL NOTE

As you've no doubt gathered already, at Grand Central Market, food is not just about the biological necessity of eating. It's also about community, discovery, and adventure. Food at its best is an experience, and the best experiences are the ones shared with others. In that spirit, many of the recipes in this book make six to eight servings. (Some recipes, such as those for noodles, are more successful at home when made in smaller batches of four servings.)

The fun of getting into the kitchen with a new recipe is second only to the fun of sitting down to eat with family and friends. The recipes in the pages ahead are meant to inspire you to gather your own community around a shared table for breakfast, lunch, dinner, or anything in between.

BREAKFAST

EGGSLUT'S MENU IS SMALL BUT MIGHTY, REVOLVING MOSTLY AROUND BREAKFAST sandwiches on brioche buns. But the signature dish just might be the soft coddled egg with potato puree, aka the Slut. It arrives in a mason jar, and the pro move is to stir the egg and potatoes together. Scoop them out with a crunchy toasted baguette, which basically acts as an edible spork. The Slut became an instant Market classic, further testament to the incredible edible egg.

¼ cup **fine sea salt**, plus more for garnish

1 pound **russet potatoes**, peeled and cut into ¾-inch dice

10½ tablespoons **unsalted butter,** softened

Kosher salt

4 large **eggs**

2 tablespoons thinly sliced fresh **chives**

8 ¼-inch-thick slices **baguette**, cut on a diagonal, toasted

Note: *This recipe requires 4 half-pint mason jars with sealable lids.*

1

In a large stockpot, bring 7 quarts water to a rolling boil over high heat. Stir in the sea salt. Add the diced potatoes, and cook until fork-tender, 15 to 20 minutes. Turn off the heat, and remove the potatoes with a slotted spoon, reserving the water in the pot. Run the potatoes through a food mill or ricer until smooth. Stir in the butter. Add kosher salt to taste.

2

Transfer the potato puree to a piping bag (or zip-top plastic bag with the corner snipped off) and divide it evenly among 4 half-pint mason jars, filling each about one-third of the way. Crack an egg into each jar on top of the puree, and seal the lids.

3

Return the water on the stove to a simmer over medium-high heat. Place the jars in the simmering water and cook for 15 minutes, or until the egg whites are set.

4

Remove the jars from the water, and take off the lids. Garnish each with a sprinkle of chives and sea salt. Serve with the toasted baguette alongside for scooping.

SERVES 4

THE slut

(CODDLED EGGS WITH POTATO PUREE)

LATE IN 2012, WORD STARTED GETTING AROUND LA THAT A

classically trained chef named Alvin Cailan had ditched fine dining to sell breakfast sandwiches out of a food truck. The name of the truck was . . . unexpected, to say the least. *Eggslut*. What did it mean? No one knew, but before long, fans were making their breakfast plans based on Eggslut's Twitter feed. Knowing its location was like the ultimate insider information for serious LA food fans. Consider this post from @RuthBourdain, a parody mash-up of Ruth Reichl and Anthony Bourdain:

Magical moon this morning: Jonathan Gold's ample behind pressed against my window. Tangerine-scented air. Back in LA. Where's Eggslut?

People found Eggslut and loved its egg sandwiches handed out through the truck's window. The Fairfax piled soft-scrambled eggs on a brioche bun with melted Cheddar cheese and caramelized onions. The fried-egg-bacon-and-cheese sandwich with chipotle ketchup dripped when you bit into it. Alvin designed his food to look good on Instagram—and it did. The first time you went to Eggslut, it probably crossed your mind that this was the best reinvention of breakfast since the Egg McMuffin.

Alvin and his business partner Jeff Vales visited GCM and saw the potential immediately. They zeroed in on an empty stall at the Market's Broadway entrance, only a few feet from the sidewalk. The abandoned space felt raw and gritty as traffic barreled down Broadway. But that was where Alvin wanted to build his first fixed location.

"I serve food out of a truck," he explained. "I'm on the street. I want to stay on the street."

Alvin met Adele and impressed her with his business savvy. Eggslut's name was provocative, but his demeanor was gentle. There was a clear and persuasive logic to this thinking.

"Why the name?" Adele asked.

"Because I love eggs," he said. "I'm a slut for eggs. Eggslut."

Business negotiations progressed rapidly. Still, a question mark lingered over the name. Every GCM vendor was required to install a neon sign in keeping with long-standing tradition. Would the name "Eggslut" be too high voltage for a family-friendly food hall? The team debated; Adele decided.

"Let 'em keep the name," said Adele. "Everybody will remember it."

And they have. Almost since the day it opened, Eggslut has been the Market's busiest vendor. Hour-long lines of one hundred people are not unusual. Insider tip: The shortest wait times are Mondays and Tuesdays between 9:30 and 11:30 a.m.

eggs BAKED IN MOLE

SERVES 8

LOS ANGELES IS A NATIONAL HOT SPOT FOR CULINARY EXPERIMENTS BECAUSE OF the city's cultural diversity. Roy Choi, a Korean guy who grew up in a neighborhood with a large Mexican population, put kimchi on carne asada to create the Kogi taco (and launch an empire). Vendors at GCM are likewise tweaking traditions: smoked brisket tacos, *siete mares* soup with dashi, vegan ramen. This recipe for eggs baked in mole—the famous sauce of ground nuts, chiles, and spices from Oaxaca, Mexico—isn't trying to be authentically Oaxacan, so the garnishes you choose will make it authentic to you. You can bake the eggs in a single large dish or in individual ramekins.

1 teaspoon **vegetable oil** or **lard**, plus more for the pan

1 teaspoon dried Mexican **oregano**

½ teaspoon **cumin seeds**, toasted

½ teaspoon dried **red chile flakes**

1 teaspoon smoked **paprika**

¼ teaspoon freshly ground **black pepper**

1 teaspoon **kosher salt**

6 tablespoons **mole poblano paste**

1½ cups **chicken** or **vegetable stock** or **water**

6 **corn tortillas**, store-bought or homemade (page 77), warmed

8 large **eggs**

½ cup grated **Monterey Jack cheese**

¼ cup grated **Parmesan cheese**

GARNISHES

2 **scallions**, whites and greens, thinly sliced

2 tablespoons chopped fresh **cilantro**

Zest of ½ **lime**

Toasted **sesame seeds**

1 **avocado**, peeled and sliced, for serving

Note: *There's a wide range of moles out there, from green to dark and chocolaty. This recipe calls for mole poblano, which is very slightly sweet, to balance the heat of chiles and the subtle nuttiness* of ground sesame seeds. Mole poblano paste is sold at GCM by Chiles Secos and Valeria's, and is available online and in the grocery store's ethnic aisles.

1
Preheat the oven to 350°F. Lightly oil or grease with lard a 9 × 9-inch baking dish, a cazuela, or 8 individual ramekins.

2
Combine the oregano, cumin, chile flakes, paprika, black pepper, and salt in a mortar, spice blender, or food processor. Crush, but do not grind the spice blend too finely.

3
Heat the oil in a small saucepan over medium heat. When the oil shimmers, add the mole paste. When it begins to melt, stir it around with a whisk. Let it sizzle for about a minute, then pour in ¼ cup of the stock while whisking vigorously; it will be absorbed by the paste almost immediately. Whisk in a bit more stock. When that's incorporated and the sauce starts to bubble at the edges and thicken, whisk in more stock. Keep going until you have added all the stock, then allow the sauce to bubble and thicken, 3 to 5 minutes. The consistency should be somewhere between a pancake batter and a milk shake. If the sauce seems too thin, just cook it down for a few minutes more, stirring frequently. If it's too thick, stir in another tablespoon or two of stock.

4
Line the prepared baking dish with the warm tortillas so that they overlap slightly. (If using individual ramekins, cut the tortillas into quarters, and line the ramekins with the tortilla pieces.) Pour the mole over the tortillas.

5
One at a time, crack the eggs into a small bowl, and tip them into the mole so that they don't touch. Sprinkle them evenly with 2 teaspoons of the prepared spice blend. Add a thin layer of grated Monterey Jack. Top with the grated Parmesan. Transfer to the oven and bake until the eggs are just set, 10 to 12 minutes.

6
Garnish with the sliced scallions, cilantro, lime zest, and toasted sesame seeds. Serve with the avocado alongside.

PAN DULCE

CLARK STREET OWNER ZACK HALL CALLS THIS *"PAN DULCE, SORT OF."* GRAND Central Market—like all of Los Angeles—has a rich Latin culinary heritage, and Zack remembers that when he first moved into the Market in late 2014, a question he heard repeatedly from customers was, *"Tienes pan dulce?"* In his head, he thought, "This is a French bakery. We have baguette!" Then he decided to make his own French-Mexican mash-up of the sweet, bready Mexican treat using brioche buns. Think of it as a grown-up variation on cinnamon toast.

1 cup (2 sticks) **unsalted butter**

¾ cup **sugar**

2½ tablespoons ground **cinnamon**

Pinch of **sea salt**

12 **brioche rolls** or other soft buns, warmed

1 Melt the butter in a small saucepan over low heat. In a large bowl, mix together the sugar, cinnamon, and salt.

2 Brush the buns with the butter and roll them, one at time, through the sugar mixture until completely coated. That's it.

SERVES 12

BOSTOCK IS NEXT-LEVEL TOAST, MADE IN THIS VERSION FROM CLARK STREET
Bread with thick slices of day-old brioche or challah. Because it's sweet and sort of fancy—here, baked with a topping of almond cream and Meyer lemon marmalade—bostock could fill the role of French toast at a sit-down brunch. But it also travels well and is tidy enough to eat with your hands, so you could take a batch with you somewhere, like you would a box of doughnuts.

Meyer lemons are thought to be a hybrid between the true lemon and the orange. They arrived in California from China over one hundred years ago and, until recently, were virtually unknown outside the state. Their taste is milder and sweeter than that of regular sour lemons.

MEYER LEMON BOSTOCK

SERVES
8

1 cup (2 sticks) **unsalted butter**, softened

1½ cups granulated **sugar**

4 large **eggs**, lightly beaten

1 cup **almond meal**

1 loaf day-old **brioche** or **challah**, cut into 8 1-inch-thick slices

½ cup **Meyer lemon marmalade**, store-bought or homemade (recipe follows)

½ cup sliced **almonds**

Confectioners' sugar, for dusting

Note: *For the sake of time management, you can make the almond cream in advance. It will keep in the refrigerator in an airtight container for up to 3 days.*

1

Preheat the oven to 425°F.

2

Make the almond cream: In a large bowl, cream the butter and 1 cup of the sugar with an electric mixer until smooth. Add the eggs and whip. Slowly add the almond meal, mixing until fully incorporated.

3

Make a simple syrup: Combine the remaining ½ cup sugar and ½ cup water in a small saucepan over medium heat. Stir until the sugar dissolves. Remove the pan from the heat.

4

Lay out the bread on a parchment-lined baking sheet. Brush one side of each slice liberally with the simple syrup. Spread 2 tablespoons of the almond cream over each slice from edge to edge. Spread 1 tablespoon of the marmalade over each slice. Sprinkle the sliced almonds on top, and lightly press them down to stick.

5

Transfer the baking sheet to the oven and bake the bostock until the almond cream is cooked through and the tops are lightly browned, 20 to 25 minutes. Remove from the oven and cool on a rack. Dust with confectioners' sugar and serve.

RECIPE CONTINUES

SIMPLIFIED
MEYER LEMON MARMALADE

MARKET RECIPE

1½ pounds **Meyer lemons**

1½ cups **sugar**

Fresh **lemon juice** or **honey**, as needed

1

Scrub the lemons under hot water to strip any wax from their peels. Using a vegetable peeler, remove the zest, leaving behind the white pith. Cut the peels into fine strips. Using a sharp knife, trim the white pith from the lemons and discard. Cut the lemon pulp into ¼-inch dice. Discard any seeds.

2

Combine the peel, pulp, and 1½ cups water in a medium nonreactive saucepan over high heat. Bring to a boil, then reduce the heat to low and simmer for 20 minutes, or until the peel is very soft. There should still be some liquid left. Add the sugar and stir to dissolve. Increase the heat to high, and cook, stirring frequently, until the mixture reaches a jam-like consistency, about 20 minutes. Remove the pan from the heat, and chill a teaspoon of the hot marmalade on a small plate in the freezer for 1 minute. Taste and adjust the sweet-tart balance as needed by adding fresh lemon juice or a drizzle of honey to the pot. If the chilled marmalade is runny, return the pot to the stove and cook over medium heat for 2 to 3 minutes longer.

3

Let the finished marmalade cool for 10 minutes, then stir well. Store, refrigerated, in an airtight container for up to 2 weeks.

MAKES 1 PINT

BREAKFAST BURRITO
WITH EGGS & CHORIZO

CHIQUITO MEANS "TINY" IN SPANISH, AND JOSE CHIQUITO'S STALL IS INDEED teensy, less than 200 square feet. But there's always a line at breakfast. Not long after the first new tenants opened at GCM in mid-2013, a young woman stepped out of the line to beg Kevin not to kick out Jose Chiquito because she loved their breakfast burrito. Obviously Jose Chiquito wasn't going anywhere—*everyone* loves the breakfast burrito. Jose Chiquito rolls the components of this recipe—eggs scrambled with chorizo and crisped hash browns—in a flour tortilla to form a burrito. If you prefer, you can divide them among warm corn tortillas to make breakfast tacos. And yes, locavores, this recipe uses American cheese. It melts and forms a sauce that brings together the other elements. If that feels wrong to you, another cheese would work, or you can leave it out entirely.

1 pound **russet potatoes**, peeled

2 tablespoons plus 2 teaspoons **vegetable oil**

Kosher salt and **pepper**

1 teaspoon **lard**

¼ pound fresh **chorizo**, store-bought or homemade (recipe follows)

8 large **eggs**, lightly beaten

8 slices **American cheese**

4 large **flour tortillas**, store-bought or homemade (page 77), warmed

Roasted Tomato Salsa (page 83) or your favorite store-bought salsa

Note: *The potatoes for the hash-brown filling require 30 minutes of drying time after prepping. Start with them. As they dry you can make the salsa or chorizo, if you want to use homemade instead of store-bought. For the sake of time management, either could also be made a day ahead.*

1

Grate the potatoes on the largest holes of a box grater. Rinse them in a bowl of cold water to remove the excess starch, and drain them well in a colander. Repeat. Squeeze the potatoes dry, first pressing them with your hands, then wringing them in a clean kitchen towel. Spread the grated potatoes on a baking sheet, and let dry for 30 minutes.

2

Heat 1 tablespoon of the oil in a large cast-iron skillet over medium heat. When the oil shimmers, add half the potatoes and press them into a thin layer with a spatula. Season generously with salt and pepper, and fry for 5 minutes, or until the bottom browns. Using a spatula, flip the potatoes over in several pieces. Fry for 4 minutes longer, or until crisped on both sides. Transfer the potatoes to a plate, and cover with foil to keep them warm. Heat another tablespoon of the oil in the skillet, and cook the remaining potatoes in the same way.

3

Melt the lard in a medium skillet over medium-high heat. Add the chorizo and fry until cooked through, about 10 minutes, stirring frequently to break up the meat. Remove from the heat.

4

Heat the remaining 2 teaspoons oil in a large sauté pan over medium heat. Add the cooked chorizo. When it begins to sizzle, add the eggs and push them around gently until they reach a soft set. Push the eggs to one side of the pan, and add the potatoes. Warm the potatoes for 30 seconds, then flip them and cook 30 seconds longer, or until heated through. Carefully fold the potatoes into the eggs, just enough to barely combine them. Lay a slice of cheese (or two!) over the top, and cover the pan. Remove the pan from the heat and set aside for about 30 seconds, until the cheese melts.

5

To assemble, moving quickly, lay a warmed tortilla on a dry surface. Spoon a quarter of the filling onto the tortilla. Fold the bottom up around the filling, tuck in the sides, and roll the burrito away from you, all the while maintaining a firm tension to ensure a tight wrap—be brave and decisive. Repeat with the remaining tortillas. Slice the burritos in half, and serve with salsa alongside.

MAKES 4 BURRITOS

CHORIZO

¼ pound ground **pork**

¼ teaspoon **cayenne pepper**

¾ teaspoon **sea salt**

1 teaspoon ground **oregano**

1 teaspoon ground **cumin**

1 teaspoon **apple cider vinegar**

1 teaspoon **sweet paprika**

1 teaspoon **lard**

Combine all the ingredients in a small bowl. Mix together with your hands until the spices are thoroughly distributed. To test the seasoning, fry a tablespoon of the mixture, taste, and adjust as needed.

MAKES 4 OUNCES

HUEVOS
RANCHEROS

HUEVOS RANCHEROS ARE NOTHING MORE THAN FRIED EGGS WITH SALSA
ranchera, traditionally served with sides of beans and rice to round out the plate. What distinguishes the Jose Chiquito version is that owner Marlon Medina serves the eggs over a bed of hot golden tortilla chips and douses the whole plate with salsa. The result is halfway to *chilaquiles,* the famous hangover cure of tortillas simmered in salsa. And as Saturday morning at the Market makes clear, a lot of bleary-eyed folks have come in for something—anything!—to ease the pain after a boozy Friday night.

6 **corn tortillas**, store-bought or homemade (page 77)

Oil, for frying

8 large **eggs**

Salsa Ranchera (page 84), or your favorite store-bought salsa

1

Cut the tortillas into wedges or strips. In a large heavy-bottomed skillet, heat ½ inch of oil over medium heat. Test the oil by dipping in the edge of a tortilla; the oil should sizzle, and small bubbles should form. Add half the tortilla pieces and fry until golden and crisp, about 2 minutes per side. Transfer to a paper-towel-lined tray to drain. Repeat with the remaining tortilla pieces. Divide the chips among 4 plates.

2

Drain the excess oil from the skillet, crack in the eggs, and fry to your liking. Slide them on top of the tortilla chips on the plates. Smother with salsa ranchera and serve.

SERVES 4

SMOKED
salmon
LATKE

WEXLER'S DELI CHEF MICAH WEXLER HAS REINVENTED THE JEWISH DELI tradition from the ground up. He cures his own pastrami in-house, he ferments his own pickles in-house, and he smokes his own fish . . . in-house. In particular, Wexler's smoked salmon is hands down the best in town—silky, supple, and sliced by hand so thinly that you can read the newspaper through it, as the old saying goes. At GCM, Wexler's serves his lox on bagels, natch. This recipe takes lox one step further with homemade latkes. It's the play-to-win breakfast and makes good on Wexler's motto, Smoke Fish Every Day.

1¼ pounds **Yukon Gold potatoes**

1 medium **white onion**

½ teaspoon **kosher salt**, plus more for water

2 large **eggs**, beaten

1 cup **all-purpose flour**

¼ teaspoon freshly ground **black pepper**

Oil, for frying

½ pound **lox**

½ cup **crème fraîche**

2 ounces black American **caviar**, such as sturgeon or paddlefish

Chopped fresh **chives**, for garnish

1

In a food processor fitted with the grating disc, grate the potatoes and onion together. Run the shredded mixture through the grating blade a second time. (You can also do this on a box grater.)

2

Bring a large pot of salted water to a boil over high heat. Add the potato-onion mixture and blanch for 45 seconds. Drain in a colander, and press to squeeze out as much water as possible. Spread the mixture on a sheet pan, and refrigerate until cool, about 15 minutes.

3

In a large bowl, combine the cooled potato-onion mixture with the eggs and flour. Season with the salt and pepper.

4

Heat ¼ inch of oil in a large cast-iron skillet over medium heat. Using your hands, shape about 2 tablespoons of the potato-onion mixture at a time into slightly flattened rounds. When the oil shimmers, carefully lower the latkes into the hot oil, working in batches and being sure not to overcrowd the pan. Cook for 3 to 4 minutes per side, or until golden and crispy. Drain on a paper-towel-lined tray.

5

To serve, transfer the latkes to a platter. Place a slice of lox, a dollop of crème fraîche, and a spoonful of caviar on top of each. Garnish with a sprinkle of chives.

SERVES 9

IN THE 1920S, the neighborhood of Boyle Heights, across the Los Angeles River from downtown, was predominantly Jewish. From then and through the next seventy years, delis always had a place at Grand Central Market. Adele remembers that when Ira bought the Market in 1984, a spot called Hillcrest was the last of the Jewish-owned delis. It closed in the 1990s because the proprietor finally retired—at ninety-three years old. A literal trace of the old business remains on the concrete floor near the Hill Street entrance, where you can still see the former stall's outline underfoot in what is now a seating area.

Adele wanted to bring the Jewish deli tradition back to GCM, and she was delighted when a proposal came in from chef Micah Wexler, a rising star in Los Angeles thanks to his former restaurant, Mezze. Wexler and his business partner, Michael Kassar, explained that they wanted to re-create the traditional Jewish deli of their childhood memories. Except that they wanted the stall to have white subway tile graffiti-ed by their art friend Gregory Siff and a hip-hop soundtrack. And that's exactly what they did.

The offerings at Wexler's Deli will be familiar to deli fans everywhere: bagels and smoked fish, pastrami sandwiches with dill pickles, roast turkey on a Kaiser roll. But the level of craft that Micah and his crew lavish on the food is almost crazy. It has certainly shaken up LA's staid deli dynasties and attracted huge crowds.

GCM: Before you opened, the GCM team jokingly called Wexler's a "neo-retro" deli. So which is it? Neo or retro?

WEXLER: Wexler's is about craftsmanship. Craftsmanship is the repetition of a technique that gets you closer and closer to perfection. That's not always in the modern chef's head, but it became an important part of my journey as a chef. From the get-go, we didn't want to do a "creative deli" or do a riff on deli.

KASSAR: We don't think about old school/ new school. This is our deli. This is an expression of our upbringing. We ate a lot of deli foods, and it means a lot in our taste memory. This is our expression of what a great deli should be: only food at the highest level, in a community setting, with hip-hop, and a collegial environment.

WEXLER: We love restaurants in general. A great restaurant is a place where the owner would like to go and hang out when not working.

GCM: I hear that, but what does hip-hop have to do with it? Or the graffiti décor, for that matter?

KASSAR: This is who we are as people. We're guys from New York and LA. We love hip-hop music. We come from the city, and deli food is urban food. The art is graffiti art. But we're not trying to be cutting edge. Our lox and pastrami is the same as if a Jewish person were doing it on the Lower East Side 100 years ago.

WEXLER: From the get-go, we wanted people to bite into a bagel and lox and say "Fuck, that's the best bagel and lox." That's the emotion we want to evoke. We want them to say that every day.

CHICKEN CHOP SUEY

EVEN BEFORE THE GCM SECURITY GUARD RINGS THE BELL TO OPEN THE MARKET, a line has usually gathered at China Cafe. By 8:10 a.m., customers fill the wraparound counter beneath the vintage signage that looks as if it had been lifted from a Mickey Spillane novel. What comes out of the crowded kitchen is not your standard breakfast fare, but steaming bowls of dumpling soup and plates heaped with chow mein and chop suey. It seems odd until you realize that some of those customers are probably coming in from their night shift at the wholesale produce markets downtown; our breakfast is their dinner. And in any case, it's easy to see the appeal of a savory, salty breakfast, especially on an overcast morning during the annual foggy spell known as June Gloom. Why are people supposed to eat only eggs or waffles before noon?

2 **chicken thighs** (about ¾ pound)

3 cups **chicken stock** or **water**

1 teaspoon **kosher salt**, plus more as needed

3 tablespoons **sunflower oil**

1 pound **bok choy**, sliced lengthwise into ribbons

Pinch of **sugar**

1 teaspoon **oyster sauce**

¼ teaspoon **toasted sesame oil**

¼ cup sliced **mushrooms**

2 teaspoons **cornstarch** mixed with 2 tablespoons **water**

Cooked rice, for serving

Lime wedges, sliced avocado, and **sriracha** or **hot sauce**, for garnish (optional)

1 In a medium saucepan, cover the chicken thighs with the chicken stock, and bring to a boil over high heat. Add ½ teaspoon of the salt, and reduce the heat to maintain a steady simmer until the chicken is cooked, about 25 minutes. Remove the chicken, reserving the broth in the pot, and set it aside to cool. Once the chicken is cool, pull off the meat with tongs or your fingers, discarding the skin and bones.

2 Heat 2 tablespoons of the sunflower oil in a large skillet over high heat. When the oil shimmers, add the bok choy, and sauté for 5 minutes. Add a scant cup of the reserved broth, and cook until the liquid has evaporated completely, about 5 minutes; it's okay for the bok choy to brown a bit. Remove the bok choy from the skillet.

3 Heat the remaining 1 tablespoon sunflower oil in the same skillet over high heat. When the oil shimmers, stir in the sugar, the remaining ½ teaspoon of salt, the oyster sauce, sesame oil, and mushrooms, and sauté for 1 minute, until the mushrooms are softened. Add the chicken, ½ cup of the reserved broth, and the cornstarch mix. Bring to a rapid boil, and add the sautéed bok choy. Stir well, and adjust the seasonings to taste.

4 Serve with rice and a small cup of the leftover broth. To go full-on GCM style, garnish with lime wedges, sliced avocado, and sriracha.

SERVES 2

COCONUT CREAM DOUGHNUTS

THE 1922 BROCHURE FOR GRAND CENTRAL PUBLIC MARKET INCLUDES A prominent advertisement from the vendor in stall C-1, Famous Cream Doughnuts. The ad's copy is almost like a fast-talking sales pitch: "Our cream doughnut formula met with instant success, for it comprised only the very best of ingredients," it reads. "Another thing, we are the only ones to eliminate the 'hole in the doughnut,' and that's the truth, too. And besides we have added to our doughnut family the CREAM COCOANUT DOUGHNUT. Try them next time."

This claim about having eliminated "the hole in the doughnut" seems dubious, at best. According to historians, the question of which came first, the doughnut or the hole, has been settled definitively. The earliest doughnuts, also called *olykoeks* in New York in the early nineteenth century, were round and solid. Historical accuracy aside, you can practically smell the scent of warm coconut cream–filled doughnuts wafting up from the ad.

Today Famous Cream Doughnuts is gone without a trace, but this recipe was inspired by that long-ago ad and, in particular, its promise that "we make them to eat, and that's the truth of the matter."

1 13½-ounce can **full-fat coconut milk**

1 cup **whole milk**

2 tablespoons **unsalted butter**, plus more for the bowl

1 **cinnamon stick**

2¼ cups plus 3 tablespoons **all-purpose flour**, plus more for rolling

¼ cup **tapioca flour**

½ teaspoon **kosher salt**

½ cup plus 2 tablespoons **granulated sugar**

1½ teaspoons **active dry yeast**

3 large **eggs**, lightly beaten

1 **egg yolk**

1½ cups sweetened **shredded coconut**

1 teaspoon **vanilla extract**

Oil, for frying

Confectioners' sugar, for dusting

1

In a small saucepan, heat 2 tablespoons of the coconut milk, the whole milk, butter, cinnamon stick, and 2 tablespoons water over low heat. When the butter has melted, remove the pan from the heat. Steep for 30 minutes. Remove and reserve the cinnamon stick.

2

In a stand mixer fitted with the paddle attachment, combine 2¼ cups of the all-purpose flour, the tapioca flour, the salt, 2 tablespoons of the granulated sugar, and the yeast. With the motor running on low, pour in the warm milk mixture and beat until incorporated, scraping down the sides as necessary.

3

Switch to the dough hook attachment. Add 1 egg, and beat on medium until the dough starts to pull away from the side of the bowl, 2 to 3 minutes. Transfer the dough to a lightly buttered large bowl, cover, and set it aside in a warm spot to rise for about an hour, or until doubled in bulk.

4

In a medium bowl, beat together the remaining ½ cup granulated sugar, 2 eggs, the egg yolk, and the remaining 3 tablespoons all-purpose flour. Heat the remainder of the coconut milk (about 1½ cups) with the shredded coconut and the reserved cinnamon stick in a small saucepan over low heat. Bring to a simmer, then remove the cinnamon stick. Pour the warm liquid over the sugar-egg mixture, and whisk to incorporate. Return the mixture to the saucepan, and set it over medium heat. Cook, stirring constantly, just until it begins to boil. Remove the pan from the heat, and add the vanilla. Transfer to a bowl, press plastic wrap directly against the surface to prevent a skin from forming, and refrigerate until set, about an hour.

5

In a Dutch oven, heat 3 inches of oil to 360°F. Gently turn the dough out onto a floured surface. Roll it out to ½-inch thickness. Using a 3- to 3½-inch cutter (or a drinking glass), cut out a dozen doughnuts. As you press into the dough, twist the cutter to seal the edges. Working in batches, fry the doughnuts until golden, 1 to 2 minutes per side. (Test one first. If it sinks, the oil isn't hot enough.) Lift out the doughnuts with a spider or a slotted spoon, and drain on a rack or a paper-towel-lined tray until cool.

6

Transfer the set filling to a pastry bag fitted with a #12 tip. Use a butter knife to make a ½-inch incision on the side of each doughnut. Without enlarging the incision, work the tip of the knife to open a pocket in the doughnut. Pipe 2 to 3 tablespoons of filling into each doughnut. Dust with confectioners' sugar and serve.

MAKES 12 DOUGHNUTS

YEASTED waffles

WHEN G&B COFFEE OPENED IN 2013, DOWNTOWN'S HISTORIC CORE DIDN'T HAVE a good coffee shop, so it didn't take long for downtowners to discover G&B's loooong walk-up bar facing Hill Street. Adele and the team got to know dozens of the regular customers—the place was like *Cheers* for caffeine. Within a year, success meant that G&B outgrew its original layout, so cofounders Kyle Glanville and Charles Babinski expanded with a wraparound counter that allowed for 360-degree service in the round. That's also when G&B installed its waffle irons. Their yeasted waffles became an overnight Market classic. Crisp and airy, they go equally well with the suggested toppings of confectioners' sugar, ricotta, and jam, or the traditional maple syrup.

1 tablespoon **active dry yeast**

2½ teaspoons **granulated sugar**

2¾ cups **whole milk**

¾ cup (1½ sticks) **unsalted butter**, melted

3½ cups **all-purpose flour**

1 teaspoon **kosher salt**

3 large **eggs**

½ scant teaspoon **baking powder**

Confectioners' sugar, **ricotta cheese**, and **raspberry jam**, store-bought or homemade (recipe follows), for serving

Note: *The batter needs to rest overnight.*

1

In a large bowl, whisk together ¾ cup warm water, the yeast, and the granulated sugar. Set aside in a warm place until bubbly, 10 minutes. Meanwhile, in a small saucepan, warm the milk over low heat. Whisk in the melted butter. In a medium bowl, combine the flour and salt. Whisk a third of the wet ingredients into the yeast mixture. Then whisk in a third of the dry ingredients. Alternate the ingredients until everything is combined and you have a smooth, thin batter. Cover the bowl tightly with plastic wrap, and leave on the counter at room temperature overnight. It will get bubbly and fragrant.

2

The next morning, preheat a waffle iron. In a small bowl, beat together the eggs and baking powder, then whisk this into the yeasted batter. Ladle the batter into the waffle iron and cook according to manufacturer's instructions, until the waffle is light brown, 2 to 3 minutes. Repeat with the remaining batter.

3

Dust with confectioners' sugar, and serve with a dollop of ricotta cheese and a spoonful of jam.

SERVES 8 TO 10

RECIPE CONTINUES

QUICK
RASPBERRY JAM
WITH ROSÉ

4 cups fresh **raspberries**

1 cup **sugar**

¼ cup **dry rosé**

1

Combine the raspberries, sugar, and wine in a
medium bowl, and crush them with a potato masher
(or your hands).

2

Transfer the mixture to large nonreactive saucepan.
Bring to a boil over high heat, stirring frequently
with a wooden spoon, then reduce the heat to
medium-high to maintain a steady boil. Stirring
constantly, cook until reduced and thickened, 8 to
10 minutes. Test the consistency by putting a
teaspoon of jam on a chilled plate in the freezer for
1 minute. If the chilled jam forms a light skin that
wrinkles when you push your finger through it, it's
ready. If not, cook for 1 minute longer and check
again.

3

Remove the pan from the heat and allow the jam to
cool. Store in an airtight container in the refrigerator
for up to 2 weeks.

MAKES 1 PINT

G&B COFOUNDERS KYLE GLANVILLE AND CHARLES BABINSKI HAVE LAUNCHED A second coffee company called Go Get 'Em Tiger since opening at GCM, but the Market location remains the duo's R&D department. It's where they first rolled out the Tumi, a noncaffeinated pick-me-up made from nut milk spiked with fresh turmeric, ginger, and honey. This recipe, which has been adapted to make at home, can be served hot or cold.

1 cup whole blanched **almonds**

½ cup whole **macadamia nuts**

⅓ cup pitted **dates**

3 ounces fresh **turmeric root**, peeled and coarsely chopped

3 ounces fresh **ginger**, peeled and coarsely chopped

3 tablespoons plus 1 teaspoon **honey**

Freshly ground **black pepper** or **cayenne pepper**

Note: *The process for making nut milk requires an overnight soak. Unused milk can be stored in the refrigerator for up to 3 days. It will separate; shake well before using.*

1

Combine the nuts and dates with 5 cups water in a large container. Cover and soak overnight at room temperature.

2

The next day, add the turmeric and ginger to the container of soaking nuts. Working in batches, if necessary, pulse the mixture in a blender or food processor for 2 minutes, until super smooth. Strain through a jelly bag or other fine-mesh bag, capturing the milk in a large bowl. Alternatively, line a colander set over a large bowl with a double thickness of cheesecloth that has been wetted and wrung out, and pour the liquids through the cloth. Either way, squeeze the grounds fiercely to extract every drop, then discard the grounds. Add the honey to the milk in the bowl, and stir to dissolve. Add pepper to taste.

3

If desired, heat the milk on the stovetop or in the microwave before serving.

SERVES 8

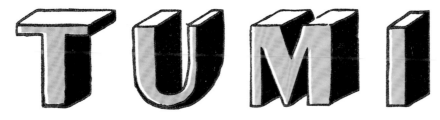

TUMI

(TURMERIC ALMOND-MACADAMIA MILK)

G&B COFOUNDERS

Kyle Glanville and Charles Babinksi spend more time these days sending e-mails than pulling espressos—they have a mini empire to run—but that doesn't mean they've stepped back from the geeky barista perfectionism that has been their calling card since day one. One morning at the Market, Charles closed his laptop for a minute to talk about what makes a coffee bar great. (Hint: It's not the coffee.)

GCM: People throw around the term "third-wave coffee," so let's just review for a moment. The first wave was the big commercial companies like Folgers, right? Second wave was Peet's and Starbucks—a step up from what came before. Now the third-wave places include G&B, Intelligensia, Stumptown, and the rest. But really, does the world need another coffee shop?

BABINSKI: [*Laughs*] We definitely thought LA needed another coffee shop because we started G&B. But what sets us apart? The thing is, we've not hung our hats on how to make coffee. We assume that knowledge is out there. If someone really loves coffee, we want to offer something for them, but that's not what makes G&B. What we have hung our hat on is a sense of exploration and trying to do the best things possible regardless of how tricky that is.

GCM: What does that mean?

BABINSKI: Our almond-macadamia milk is the best example. You know how many places make their own almond milk? Almost none. They give up because it's a pain in the ass—a lot of work. You have to just do it. It's not culinary; it's a practice. By the way, it's worth saying that what we're doing on a commercial scale is way easier to do at home, and you can adjust it as you like. But to be fair, the price of macadamia nuts is meaningful.

GCM: Has G&B's nut milk changed at all since the beginning?

BABINSKI: It has. We've tweaked the almond milk over the past two years. We wouldn't leave something on the table because it's a little bit harder. We're willing to go down any alley.

MANY COOKING TECHNIQUES RELY ON A BASIC IDEA: YOU REDUCE WATER TO intensify flavor. Think of a baked apple with its shriveled appearance and concentrated taste. The same general principle holds true for raw food preparations as well. To avoid diluting this frozen nondairy smoothie from GCM's Press Brothers Juicery, you freeze the ingredients in advance so you can skip the ice when you blend them together.

2 cups peeled, cored **pineapple** chunks

4 cups tightly packed **spinach**, washed and dried

½ medium **avocado**, pitted and peeled

3 cups **Sweet Green Juice** (recipe below)

Notes: *This recipe showcases Press Brothers' Sweet Green Juice, which you can make at home with a juicer (the recipe follows), or you could use a store-bought juice that includes pineapple, cucumber, kale, and ginger among its main ingredients, although the results will vary.*

The pineapple, spinach, and avocado should to be measured and put in the freezer the day before.

1
Combine the pineapple, spinach, and avocado a zip-top plastic bag, and place in the freezer overnight.

2
Combine the frozen ingredients and juice in a blender. Pulse until creamy, about 30 seconds. Serve in a chilled pint glass with a straw.

SWEET GREEN
JUICE

4 cups (¾-inch chunks) peeled **pineapple**

4 cups (¾-inch chunks) **cucumber**

2 cups tightly packed (torn into hand-size pieces) **kale**

¼ cup (½-inch pieces) fresh **ginger**

1
Consult the manufacturer's instructions for the operation of your particular juicer. The general technique is to feed pieces into the juicer one at a time, alternating juicy bits (cucumbers, pineapple) with more fibrous ones (kale, ginger); the juicy vegetables will flush out the fibrous pulp to keep the juicer from clogging. Fiber and froth will collect in the strainer, so use a wooden spoon to push aside the solids, allowing the juice to flow more readily. Empty the strainer when the pulp mulch completely blocks the flow. (You can save it for making soup stock or compost.)

2
Store the juice, refrigerated, in an airtight container for up to 3 days. You can also freeze Sweet Green juice—it makes excellent ice pops.

MAKES 3 CUPS

V-9 IS LIKE THAT OTHER JUICE—THE ONE THAT USES EIGHT VEGETABLES— except without the insane level of sodium that often accompanies canned goods. The celery, parsley, watercress, and garlic add flavor to the tomato base, and a little bit of beet adds a shot of antioxidants and color. V-9 juice is refreshing and filling enough to be a light snack on its own. With a few pinches of salt and dashes of Worcestershire sauce and hot sauce, V-9 becomes a delicious Bloody Mary base for a Michelada (page 166).

2½ pounds heirloom **tomatoes**

2 large **carrots**, cut into 1-inch chunks

1½ **celery stalks**, with leaves, cut into 1-inch chunks

½ medium **red beet,** cut into 1-inch chunks

4 cups tightly packed **spinach**

5 cups tightly packed **romaine lettuce**

3 sprigs fresh **parsley**

½ bunch live **watercress**, leaves only

1 whole **garlic clove**, peeled

1

Consult the manufacturer's instructions for the operation of your particular juicer. The general technique is to feed pieces into the juicer one at a time, alternating juicy bits (tomatoes, celery) with more fibrous ones (carrot, spinach); the juicy vegetables will flush out the fibrous pulp to keep the juicer from clogging. Fiber and froth will collect in the strainer, so use a wooden spoon to push aside the solids, allowing the juice to flow more readily. Empty the strainer when the pulp mulch completely blocks the flow. (You can save it for making soup stock or compost.)

2

Store the juice, refrigerated, in an airtight container for up to 3 days.

V-9 juice

SERVES 2

SOJU
BLOODY MARY

THIS BLOODY MARY RECIPE WITH ASIAN SEASONINGS HAS TWO GCM INSPIRATIONS.
The first is the Bloody Mary at Belcampo Meat Company, which replaces vodka with soju, a
low-proof distilled alcohol from Korea, because the city of LA doesn't allow hard liquor to
be served at the Market. The result is a pleasantly low-octane Bloody Mary that won't knock
you out for the day. The second inspiration is an unusual ingredient: mushroom powder.
Mushroom powder is a chef's secret ingredient because it adds an intense shot of umami,
cranking up the flavors. Think of it as umami cocaine. You can buy it at Asian groceries,
upscale health foods markets, or online.

Making your own tomato juice from whole canned San Marzano tomatoes only takes a
minute, and the results crush store-bought tomato juice. Also, don't panic when you see the
ingredient list calls for fish sauce instead of Worcestershire sauce! The fish sauce provides
another umami kick, but its flavor is actually more transparent than Worcestershire. Its
fishy essence vanishes into the rich tomato flavor.

1 28-ounce can whole **San Marzano
   tomatoes** or 16 ounces unsalted
   tomato juice

1 teaspoon **mushroom powder**

2 teaspoons **wasabi powder**

⅛ teaspoon freshly ground **black
   pepper**

¼ teaspoon **kosher salt**

1 tablespoon **sriracha sauce**, or more
   to taste

1 teaspoon **fish sauce** (we like Red
   Boat)

Juice of 1 **lime**

1 cup **soju**, **tequila**, **gin**, or **vodka**

Celery, **Giardiniere** (page 146), or
   pickled vegetables, for garnish

1

Make the tomato juice: Empty
the can of tomatoes into a blender
or food processor, and pulse
until liquefied, about 30 seconds.
Strain through a fine-mesh sieve.
You should have about 2 cups of
juice.

2

Combine the juice and all the
remaining ingredients except the
soju and garnish in a pitcher. Stir
to combine, taste, and adjust the
seasoning, if needed. Stir in the
soju.

3

Serve over ice in tall glasses and
garnish as desired.

SERVES 4

TACOS, ETC.

TOSTADA MIXTA
LA TOSTADERÍA 96

CHICKEN FLAUTAS
ROAST TO GO 98

DUCK FLAUTAS
WITH DATES & MOLE AJONJOLI
CHILES SECOS 100

CHIVO (STEWED GOAT)
ROAST TO GO 103

AL PASTOR
(SEASONED PORK)
TACOS TUMBRAS A TOMAS 104

VEGAN CRUNCHY AVOCADO TACOS
WITH CORN SALSA & CHIPOTLE
"MAYO" GOLDEN ROAD BREWING 106

SPINACH & CHEESE PUPUSAS WITH CURTIDO
SARITA'S PUPUSERIA 108

Maria
Comida Mexicana

TACOS	$ 3.50	FLAUTAS TACO DORADO	$ 6.00
SOPES	$ 3.50	BURRITOS	$ 7.50
TORTAS	$ 7.50	HUARACHES	$ 7.50
TORTA CUBANA	$ 8.50	QUESADILLAS	$ 5.50
TOSTADAS	$ 5.00	CHILES RELLENOS	$ 7.50
GORDITAS	$ 5.00	COMBINATION PLATES	$ 10.00

Rice & Beans $ 8.00
All Meat $ 8.50
Meat $ 8.00
YOUR CHOICE

| ASADA Beef | POLLO Chicken | CARNITAS Pork | BUCHE Hog Maw | AL PASTOR Marinated Pork |
| LENGUA Beef Tongue | CHILE RELLENO Stuffed Chili | | CHICHARRON Pork Skin | DESEBRADA Shredded Beef |

EXTRA : Guacamole $.75   Queso $.75

SODAS M $ 1.50   L $ 2.50   refill 1/2 price
COKE · DIET COKE · FANTA · SPRITE · LEMONADE
Sodas de Botella $ 2.50
Botella de Agua $ 1.50

AGUAS M $ 1.50   L $ 2.50
HORCHATA · TAMARINDO · JAMAICA · ORANGE BANG
FLAVOR of the Day M $ 1.50   L $ 2.50

HANDMADE TORTILLAS 101

★ ★ ★

IF YOU'VE BEEN USING STORE-BOUGHT TORTILLAS ALL YOUR LIFE. GET READY TO TRANSFORM YOUR TACO GAME.

T'S LIKE THE DIFFERENCE between a sandwich on presliced, plastic-packed bread and one made with a hand-sliced, fresh-from-the-oven *boule*. Working up a batch of tortillas takes less time than driving to the store to buy them.

Claudia Armendariz of Chiles Secos taught a tortilla-making workshop at GCM's 2015 Bread Festival, which proved so popular that she brought it back the next year. The corn- and flour-tortilla recipes here come from Claudia, and the instructions are based on the techniques she taught at the festival. To make corn tortillas, you'll need masa harina, a special flour made from corn slaked with lime. It's available at any Latin market and from Bob's Red Mill; cornmeal cannot be substituted.

Making flour tortillas differs slightly from making corn tortillas. You work a little lard into the flour before adding the water to make a stiff dough, almost like a cookie dough. The lard keeps the tortilla pliable. For that reason, flour tortillas can be rolled out larger and thinner than corn tortillas. At GCM, vendors use extra-large flour tortillas for rolling burritos. Corn tortillas are the basis for homemade chips and *chilaquiles*. In general, however, when it comes to tacos, the choice of corn or flour tortillas is largely a matter of personal taste.

One note: As with most simple kitchen skills, making tortillas takes a minute to learn and a lifetime to master. A tortilla press is handy for flattening the dough, but it's not essential. You can also roll out the dough with a rolling pin, or just pat it flat against your palm. Even a funny-looking, irregular tortilla will taste delicious.

Leftover tortillas can be used for chips or tostadas. Leave them uncovered on the counter overnight to stale, then fry them in oil until crisp. You'll never buy tortilla chips from the snack aisle again.

CORN
TORTILLAS

2¼ cups **masa harina**
½ teaspoon **kosher salt**

1

Place the masa in a medium bowl and sprinkle with the salt. Pour 1½ cups hot water over, and stir it in with your hand, using a motion that simultaneously scoops the sticky dough into a mass. Knead the dough lightly in the bowl until it becomes less sticky as the water is absorbed, about 1 minute. Shape the dough into a ball, and cover the bowl with a clean kitchen towel. Set aside for 30 minutes to let the dough rest.

2

To shape the tortillas, roll about 2 tablespoons of dough (1 ounce) into a ball. Place the ball between two sheets of plastic—the best is a resealable zip-top plastic bag that has been cut open along the side seams. Using a tortilla press, a rolling pin, or your hands, flatten the dough to ⅛-inch thickness, about 5 inches in diameter. Stack the finished tortillas as you work, and keep them covered with a damp kitchen towel.

3

Heat a comal, griddle, or large cast-iron skillet over high heat. When the pan smokes, add the tortillas, working in batches, and toast them for about 1 minute per side. Stack the hot tortillas and wrap them in a clean kitchen towel. Use the tortillas warm.

MAKES ABOUT 24 5-INCH TORTILLAS

FLOUR
TORTILLAS

2¼ cups **all-purpose flour**, plus more for rolling
1 teaspoon **kosher salt**
1 teaspoon **baking powder**
4½ tablespoons **lard**

1

Combine the flour, salt, and baking powder in a large bowl. Work the lard into the flour by rubbing it between your fingertips and thumbs, then lightly rolling a handful of flour between your palms. When fully incorporated, the lard should be indistinguishable from the flour. Pour in ⅔ cup hot water, and incorporate with your hands to form a dough. Knead the dough in the bowl until it becomes less sticky. Cover the bowl with a clean kitchen towel, and set aside for 30 minutes to rest.

2

Divide the dough evenly into 8 equal-size balls. Working on a lightly floured surface, roll out each ball to ⅛-inch thickness and about 9 inches in diameter.

3

Heat a comal, griddle, or large cast-iron skillet over high heat. When the pan smokes, add the tortillas, working in batches, and toast for about 40 seconds per side. Stack the hot tortillas and wrap them in a clean towel. Use warm.

MAKES 8 9-INCH TORTILLAS

CHIPS & TOSTADAS

Day-old **corn tortillas,** store-bought or homemade
  (page 77)
Oil, for frying

1

To make chips, fold each tortilla in half, and tear it
along the seam. Repeat, folding the two halves in half
again, and tearing each tortilla into quarters. Lay the
pieces in a single layer on a baking sheet, and leave
them out, uncovered, overnight until they are totally
dried out. To make tostadas, spread whole tortillas in
a single layer on a baking sheet, and leave them out,
uncovered, overnight to dry out.

2

Heat ¼ inch of oil in a large cast-iron skillet over
high heat. When the oil shimmers, add as many
chips or tostadas as will fit in a single layer. Fry until
golden crisp, about 2 minutes per side. Remove to a
paper-towel-lined tray to drain.

3

Once cool, store the chips or tostadas in an airtight
container for up to 3 days.

QUESADILLAS

4 **corn tortillas**, store-bought or homemade (page 77)
1 ounce **queso fresco** or **Monterey Jack cheese**, cut into
  thin slices
1 **jalapeño**, sliced into ¼-inch rounds

1

Heat a comal, griddle, or large cast-iron skillet over
high heat. When the pan smokes, add the tortillas,
working in batches, and heat for 1 minute per side.
Using tongs, turn the tortillas over.

2

When the tortilla is on the second side, layer the
cheese and 3 or 4 jalapeño slices on one half. Fold
over the other half, and cook until the cheese is
melted, about 2 minutes per side. Serve hot.

SERVES 2

A TACO DE NADA, or a "nothing taco," is exactly
what it sounds like: a warm tortilla served plain. It's the best
way to appreciate the tortilla flavor, or it's a quick bite to
keep you from starving while you finish cooking the rest. A
plain tortilla could also be called a *taco de sel,* a "salt taco,"
the idea being that it's seasoned by the sweat of your palm
when you roll it.
   A nothing taco doesn't have to be entirely empty. You
could dress it up with a spoonful of salsa or mole. See page 45
for instructions on making mole poblano from paste or page 221
for green mole from scratch.

GORDITAS

Gordita means "little fatty" in Spanish. It's a corn cake, thicker than a tortilla, stuffed with beans, meat, shredded lettuce, and the usual taco garnishes. Several vendors at GCM sell gorditas, including Tacos Tumbras a Tomas and Roast to Go. *Los Angeles Times* food critic Jonathan Gold tweeted at the start of the Market's revitalization in 2014, "If they touch Roast to Go, I will be down there with a machete. #gorditas." Roast to Go is still there and still selling gorditas. Not necessarily because of @theJGold's threat, but because the gorditas draw a crowd.

The technique for gorditas is much the same as for corn tortillas, except the gorditas are rolled out a bit thicker. After baking on the comal, the gordita is fried to puff it up, forming an inner pocket like a pita.

2¼ cups **masa harina**

½ teaspoon **kosher salt**

1 tablespoon **baking powder**

2 tablespoons **lard**

1½ cups **hot water**

Oil, for frying

Beans, **meat**, **shredded lettuce**, **tomato**, **onion**, **salsa**, and **crema**, for filling

Note: *These are best enjoyed hot, as they're the easiest to work with, but if you want to make them in advance, they'll hold up—just don't slice them open until you're ready to serve.*

1

Place the masa in a medium bowl and sprinkle with the salt and baking powder. Work in the lard, first rubbing it into the masa between your fingertips and thumbs, then by rolling it between your palms. When fully incorporated, the lard should be indistinguishable from the masa. Pour the hot water over the mixture, and stir it in with your hand, using a motion that simultaneously scoops the sticky dough into a mass. Knead it lightly in the bowl until it becomes less sticky as the water is absorbed, about 1 minute. Shape the dough into a ball and cover the bowl with a clean kitchen towel. Set the dough aside to rest for 30 minutes.

2

Divide the dough evenly into 12 portions. Keeping them covered so they don't dry out, and working with one at a time, roll each into a ball. Place the ball between two sheets of plastic—the best is a resealable zip-top bag that has been cut open along the side seams. Using a tortilla press, the bottom of a glass pie plate, or a flat-bottomed pan, flatten it to a thickness of ¼ inch. If the dough cracks while shaping it, dip your hands in water and knead the dough ball a bit before reshaping it.

3

Heat a comal, griddle, or large cast-iron skillet over high heat. When it smokes, toast 2 gorditas at a time until dry to the touch and lightly toasted on one side, less than 2 minutes. Flip and toast the other side, about 2 minutes more.

4

Heat 2 inches of oil in a large cast-iron skillet over high heat to 350°F. (If you don't have a thermometer, test the oil by dropping in a small pellet of masa dough. The oil should sizzle and small bubbles should form immediately on the dough.) Fry the gorditas, one at a time, until brown and crisp, about 1 minute per side. Drain them on a paper-towel-lined tray. As soon as they're cool enough to handle, cut halfway around the edge of each gordita, creating a pita-like pocket.

5

Stuff each gordita with beans, the meat of your choice, shredded lettuce, diced tomato, diced onion, salsa, and crema.

MAKES ABOUT 12 GORDITAS

IT'S STRETCHING THE TRUTH A BIT TO SAY the recipes that follow represent *all* the salsas, because there could never be a complete list of the infinite combinations of chiles, spices, and vegetables that go into Mexico's signature condiments. While the common thread is chiles, fresh or dried, the level of spiciness ranges from subtle to fierce. Even within a single style of salsa there are more variations than first meet the eye. Is that red salsa made with dried chiles de árbol or dried chiles japonés? Or maybe with fresh cayenne? Are the tomatoes roasted? Is the flavor sharpened with vinegar? Was a sinus-piercing fresh habañero chile blended in? Salsas, as simple as they are, express a complex layering of individual habits, family traditions, local preferences, regional practices, and national customs.

All that said, the collection here provides an overview of the range of salsas served at GCM. Every taco stall in the Market offers the option of red (spicy hot) or green (comparatively mild), so versions of each are included, along with a few family recipes that vendors shared from their home kitchens.

A quick rundown of the options to get you oriented: The Red Salsa from Roast to Go, made with dried chiles de árbol and Roma tomatoes, is typical. It could be served with any taco you like. The Habañero Salsa from Tacos Tumbras a Tomas, another red salsa, highlights the fresh habañero's fruity taste and intense heat. It pairs particularly well with Al Pastor tacos (page 104).

Green Salsa (Cooked) from Roast to Go is mellower and smoother than the bright, sharp-edged Green Salsa (Uncooked) from Torres Produce. Like red salsa, the green salsas could go with anything.

Jose Chiquito's two salsas include the smoky and moderately hot Roasted Tomato—good for dipping chips—and a Salsa Ranchera, which is milder and perfect for breakfast.

More specialized are the Salsa Morita from Valeria's, made with smoky, very hot morita chiles—dried chipotles could be substituted—and the Salsa Negra from Villa Moreliana. The latter, a salsa for carnitas, is a family heirloom recipe from owner Fernando Villagomez, who had to call up his mother to get his grandmother's version of an even older family recipe that's at least one hundred years old, he says.

Next come two chunky salsas—the classic fresh Pico de Gallo and Golden Road's Corn Salsa—and a recipe for Avo Puree from Fernando's other stall, La Tostadería. The puree is a smooth, refined guacamole that Fernando created for fish tacos, but it would work just as well on chicken, vegetables, or meat tacos.

RED
SALSA

- 2 ounces (2½ cups) dried **chiles de árbol**, stems removed
- 3 **Roma tomatoes**, coarsely chopped
- 1 **garlic clove**
- ¼ teaspoon **cumin seeds**
- ⅛ teaspoon freshly ground **black pepper**
- ½ teaspoon **white vinegar**

1

Combine the chiles, tomatoes, garlic, cumin, pepper, vinegar, and 3 cups water in a small saucepan. Bring to a boil over high heat, then reduce the heat to low, and simmer until the chiles are soft, 15 to 20 minutes. Remove the pan from the heat to cool for 15 minutes.

2

Transfer the chiles and the cooking liquid to a blender or food processor, and pulse until smooth. Refrigerate unused salsa in an airtight container for up to 3 days.

MAKES 3½ CUPS

HABAÑERO
SALSA

- 2 **Roma tomatoes**, coarsely chopped
- 4 **habañero chiles**, seeded
- 1 **garlic clove**
- ¼ medium **white onion**
- ½ teaspoon **cumin seeds**
- ½ teaspoon dried **Mexican oregano**
- ½ teaspoon freshly ground **black pepper**
- 1 teaspoon fine **sea salt**
- 1 tablespoon **rice vinegar**
- 1 teaspoon **vegetable oil**

1

Combine the tomatoes, chiles, garlic, onion, cumin, oregano, black pepper, salt, vinegar, and 1½ cups water in a small saucepan. Bring to a boil over high heat, then reduce the heat to medium, and simmer until the tomatoes are collapsing, about 10 minutes. Transfer to a blender or food processor, and pulse until liquefied.

2

Heat the oil in a small saucepan over medium heat. When the oil shimmers, add the puree and boil until slightly thickened, 5 minutes, stirring occasionally. Refrigerate unused salsa in an airtight container overnight.

MAKES 1¾ CUPS

GREEN
SALSA
(COOKED)

- ½ pound **tomatillos**, hulled and quartered
- ½ pound fresh **jalapeños**, stemmed and coarsely chopped
- 1 **garlic clove**
- 1 teaspoon **cumin seeds**
- 1 teaspoon **kosher salt**
- 1 tablespoon minced fresh **cilantro**

1

Combine the tomatillos, jalapeños, garlic, cumin, salt, and 1 cup water in a small saucepan. Bring to a boil over high heat, then reduce the heat to medium, and simmer until the jalapeños are softened and dull green, 15 to 20 minutes. Remove the pan from the heat to cool for 15 minutes.

2

Transfer the mixture to a blender or food processor and pulse until smooth. Add the cilantro, pulse briefly to combine. Refrigerate unused salsa in an airtight container overnight.

MAKES 2½ CUPS

TORRES PRODUCE
STALL
D-7

GREEN
SALSA
(UNCOOKED)

1 pound **tomatillos**, hulled

8 fresh **jalapeños**, stemmed

2 fresh **serrano chiles**, stemmed

3 fresh **cilantro** sprigs

1 teaspoon freshly squeezed **lime juice**, plus more as needed

¼ teaspoon **cumin seeds**, toasted and ground

Pinch of dried **Mexican oregano**

¾ teaspoon **kosher salt**

⅛ teaspoon freshly ground **black pepper**

1

Preheat the broiler. Arrange the tomatillos, jalapeños, and serranos in a single layer on a baking sheet, and broil until softened and charred, 8 to 10 minutes. Remove the baking sheet from the oven and let cool for 5 minutes.

2

Transfer the tomatillos and chile peppers to a blender or food processor. Add the cilantro, lime juice, cumin, oregano, salt, black pepper, and ¼ cup water. Pulse until smooth. Taste and adjust the balance with more lime juice, if needed. Refrigerate unused salsa in an airtight container overnight.

MAKES 3 CUPS

JOSE CHIQUITO
STALL
A-6

ROASTED TOMATO
SALSA

6 fresh **cayenne peppers**, stemmed

7 **Roma tomatoes**, halved lengthwise

½ medium **white onion**, chopped

½ **green bell pepper**, chopped

2 **garlic cloves**

½ teaspoon **kosher salt**

1 tablespoon **vegetable oil**

1

Preheat the broiler.

2

To moderate the heat, slice the cayenne peppers lengthwise and discard some or all of the seeds. Arrange the cayenne peppers, tomatoes, onion, and bell pepper, cut-side down, in a single layer on a foil-lined baking sheet. Tuck in the garlic gloves. Transfer to the oven, and broil until the vegetables are charred and blackened in spots, about 10 minutes. Remove from the oven and let cool for 15 minutes.

3

Finely mince a tablespoon or so of the onion and garlic, and set them aside. Combine the remaining onion and garlic and the charred vegetables in a blender or food processor. Add the salt, and pulse until smooth, adding up to ½ cup water, a tablespoon at a time, until the desired consistency is reached.

4

Heat the oil in a large cast-iron skillet over high heat. When the oil shimmers, add the reserved minced onion and garlic and sauté for 1 minute, just long enough to give some flavor to the oil. Pour the salsa into the hot skillet and bring to a boil. Simmer for 5 minutes, stirring frequently. Remove from the heat and let cool before serving. Refrigerate unused salsa in an airtight container overnight.

MAKES 2½ CUPS

SALSA RANCHERA

7 **Roma tomatoes**, halved lengthwise

5 **serrano chiles**, halved lengthwise, stemmed and seeded

2 **garlic cloves**

2 tablespoons **vegetable oil**

½ medium **yellow onion**, minced

1 teaspoon fine **sea salt**

10 fresh **parsley sprigs**, minced

1

Preheat the broiler. Arrange the tomatoes and chiles, cut-side down, in a single layer on a foil-lined baking sheet. Tuck in the garlic gloves. Broil until the vegetables are charred and blackened in spots, about 10 minutes. Remove from the oven and let cool for 15 minutes.

2

Mince half a clove of the garlic, and set it aside. Transfer the remaining garlic and the roasted vegetables to a blender or food processor and pulse briefly until coarsely pureed. This salsa shouldn't be completely smooth.

3

Heat the oil in a large saucepan over medium-high heat. When it shimmers, add the reserved minced garlic, the onion, and the salt. Stir until fragrant, about 2 minutes. Pour in the pureed vegetables and bring to a boil. Reduce the heat to low, add the parsley, and simmer for 5 minutes, stirring frequently. Refrigerate unused salsa in an airtight container overnight.

MAKES 2½ CUPS

SALSA NEGRA

5 dried **chiles de árbol**

5 dried **guajillo chiles**

1 12-ounce bottle **Mexican beer**, such as Pacífico

1 **garlic clove**

1 teaspoon **chicken bouillon powder**, preferably Knorr

4 whole **black peppercorns**

1 teaspoon dried **Mexican oregano**

½ teaspoon **cumin seeds**, toasted

2 whole **cloves**

1 tablespoon **vegetable oil**

½ teaspoon **kosher salt**

1

Heat a large skillet over high heat. When it smokes, add the chiles. Stir until fragrant, less than 30 seconds per side. Remove from the heat and discard the stems. Transfer to a small bowl and pour the beer over them. Let soak for 15 minutes.

2

Transfer the chiles and beer to a blender or food processor. Add the garlic, bouillon powder, peppercorns, oregano, cumin, and cloves. Pulse until smooth.

3

Heat the oil in a medium saucepan over high heat. When it shimmers, add the pureed chiles. Reduce the heat to medium, and cook for 3 minutes, or until excess liquid has evaporated. Add the salt. Taste and adjust the seasonings. Remove from the heat and let cool to room temperature. Refrigerate unused salsa in an airtight container for up to 3 days.

MAKES 1¼ CUPS

PICO DE GALLO

4 **Roma tomatoes**, cut into ¼-inch dice

½ medium **white onion**, cut into ¼-inch dice

2 fresh **jalapeños**, stemmed and cut into ¼-inch dice

1 fresh **serrano chile**, stemmed and thinly sliced

¼ cup chopped fresh **cilantro**

½ teaspoon **kosher salt**

⅛ teaspoon freshly ground **black pepper**

1 tablespoon freshly squeezed **lime juice**

In a medium bowl, combine the tomatoes, onion, half the chiles, the cilantro, salt, black pepper, and lime juice. Taste, and adjust the spiciness with the remaining chiles, if desired. Use immediately.

MAKES 3 CUPS

VALERIA'S
STALL
D-6

SALSA MORITA

¼ cup **extra-virgin olive oil**

¼ pound dried **morita chiles**, stemmed, or dried chipotles

3 **garlic cloves**, coarsely chopped

1 teaspoon **kosher salt**

1
Heat the olive oil in a large skillet over medium heat. When it shimmers, add the whole chiles and garlic, and fry for 3 minutes, or until the garlic is well browned and the chiles inflate.

2
Transfer the chiles, garlic, and cooking oil to a blender or food processor. Add the salt and 2 cups water. Let soak for 15 minutes, then pulse until combined—it should remain a bit grainy. Let cool before serving. Refrigerate unused salsa in an airtight container for up to 3 days.

MAKES 2½ CUPS

GOLDEN ROAD BREWING
STALL
A-9

CORN SALSA

2 **red bell peppers**

2 ears of **corn**

½ **red onion**, finely diced

1 bunch fresh **cilantro**, coarsely chopped

Juice of 4 **limes**

Kosher salt and freshly ground **black pepper**

1
Roast the bell peppers over an open flame or under the broiler until the skins are completely blackened and wrinkled. Wrap them in aluminum foil, and let cool for 15 minutes. Rub off the skins, halve each, and remove and discard the seeds. Cut the peppers into ¼-inch dice. Place in a medium bowl.

2
Char the corn on the grill or in a dry skillet over high heat. Slice the kernels off the cob into the bowl with the peppers. Add the onion, cilantro, and lime juice. Toss to combine. Season with salt and pepper. Use immediately.

MAKES 3 CUPS

LA TOSTADERÍA
STALL
E-10

AVO PUREE

5 ripe **avocados**, pitted and peeled

1 teaspoon **vegetable oil**

½ fresh **jalapeño**

½ fresh **serrano chile**

15 fresh **cilantro** sprigs, chopped

2 teaspoons grated peeled **fresh ginger**

2 tablespoons freshly squeezed **lime juice**

1 teaspoon **kosher salt**

Combine the avocados, oil, chiles, cilantro, ginger, lime juice, salt, and ¼ cup water in a blender or food processor. Pulse until smooth and whipped. Refrigerate unused puree in an airtight container overnight.

MAKES 3 CUPS

CARNE ASADA IS A CORNERSTONE TACO AT GCM. EVERY TACO VENDOR WHO SELLS carne asada sells them in quantity. The catchall name, which simply means "grilled meat," disguises the fact that the specific cut of beef makes a difference. This recipe from Tacos Tumbras a Tomas calls for steak from the chuck roll, such as the Denver cut. The flat-iron steak, cut from the adjacent shoulder clod, would also work well. Both are flavorful, fairly lean, and less expensive than rib-eye and strip steaks. Both also benefit from being thinly sliced across the grain before serving—perfect for tacos. (Flank steak is a good substitute.)

2 pounds **chuck steak**, such as Denver or flat iron (flank steak could substitute)

2 **garlic cloves**, minced

½ teaspoon **kosher salt**

Freshly ground **black pepper**

Red Salsa (page 82) , or your favorite store-bought salsa, for serving

Note: *Carne asada should be marinated for at least 2 hours, preferably longer. As the name suggests, the meat should be grilled, ideally over coals. Searing it in a red-hot cast-iron skillet would be an acceptable alternative.*

1

Rub the meat with the garlic and salt. Season generously with pepper, cover, and marinate in the refrigerator for at least 2 hours, preferably overnight.

2

Preheat the grill. Pat the steaks dry with paper towels, and grill them over hot coals until well charred, about 5 minutes, then flip and cook for 3 minutes more for medium-rare, or grill to your desired doneness. Remove and let rest for 10 minutes. Thinly slice across the grain, and serve with salsa.

SERVES 8

★★★ CARNITAS

SERVES 8

WITH NO DISRESPECT TO ANY OTHER TACO AT GRAND CENTRAL MARKET, THE carnitas taco from Villa Moreliana might be the single best emblem of GCM's taco culture. At the very least, there is no porkier option. Carnitas is a technique of simmering various cuts of pork in lard (see the sidebar on page 90). The most traditional condiment for carnitas is nothing more than pickled jalapeños—although even purists allow for a topping of sliced onions tossed with oregano, habañero, and lime juice. Other taco fans insist on a splash of red or green salsa, while Villa Moreliana owner Fernando Villagomez prefers his family recipe for Salsa Negra (page 84).

Making carnitas is a bit of a project because of the long cooking time, but it's a meal in itself, and a single batch will feed a crowd. Carnitas served on homemade corn tortillas would be the ultimate menu for a Cinco de Mayo taco party.

---

3 pounds **pork shoulder**, cut into 2-inch cubes

1½ pounds meaty **short ribs**, cut apart

½ **pig's foot** (optional)

1 whole fresh **orange**, halved

5 **garlic cloves**

2 cups (1 pound) **lard**

1 pound **pork belly**, skin removed, cut into 1-inch cubes

3 teaspoons **kosher salt**

1 large **white onion**, thinly sliced

1 fresh **habañero chile**, minced

1½ tablespoons dried **Mexican oregano**

Juice of 1 **lime**

Corn tortillas, store-bought or homemade (page 77), warmed

Salsa Negra (page 84), for serving

Pickled jalapeños, chopped fresh **cilantro**, and **lime** wedges, for garnish

---

1

Arrange the shoulder, ribs, pig's foot, if using, orange, and garlic in a large Dutch oven, packing everything in as tightly as possible. Melt the lard in a small saucepan, and pour it over the meat. Add ½ cup hot water. Bring to a boil over medium heat, and maintain a fast simmer for 45 minutes, or until the meat begins to color. Add the pork belly, and press it into the cooking liquids. Cook for an additional 45 minutes, occasionally shifting the meat in the pot for even browning, until the water has evaporated and the pork is golden and tender but not yet falling apart.

2

Add 2 teaspoons of the salt, and stir to combine. Continue browning the meat in its fat until browned and crisped on all sides. The total cooking time will be about 1 hour 45 minutes.

3

Meanwhile, in a medium bowl, combine the sliced onion, habañero, oregano, lime juice, and remaining 1 teaspoon salt. Toss to combine.

4

Using tongs or a slotted spoon, transfer the pork to a cutting board. Pull the meat from the ribs and discard the bones. Discard the bones from the pig's foot, if using. Working in batches, chop together pieces of shoulder, rib meat, belly, and a bit of skin from the foot. Spoon the meat into warm tortillas. Top with the sliced onion mixture. Serve with salsa negra, and garnish with pickled jalapeño, chopped cilantro, and lime wedges alongside.

"CARNITAS IS NOT A RECIPE," says Villa Moreliana owner Fernando Villagomez, whose stall sells nothing but the classic pork specialty, which translates roughly as "little bits of meat." What Fernando means is that carnitas is bigger than any one recipe. Instead, it's a *method* of cooking and storing pork in rendered lard. "You know confit, right?" Fernando asks, referring to the French technique for simmering duck legs, then covering them with the rendered fat for storage. "Carnitas is a confit method."

While almost every taqueria in Los Angeles serves carnitas, few do it right. Carnitas originated in the Mexican state of Michoacan—Fernando's stall takes its name from the state's colonial city of Morelia—and making real carnitas requires multiple cuts of meat, lard, and an ample cooking pot. In a *Los Angeles Magazine* story, Mexican cooking authority Bill Esparza singled out Villa Moreliana as a legit example of the tradition, explaining "it's nose-to-tail here, just like back home." Fernando uses fourteen different parts of the pig, including the shoulders, ribs, and random bits such as hearts and ears. "If you want great carnitas, you have to have at least *buche* [maw], feet, tongue, and *chicharrón* [skin]," says Fernando. The flavors of the various parts mingle during their long, slow cooking. Then the *taquero* chops all the parts together with a cleaver so that their varied textures coexist in a single bite. Carnitas gives a taste of the whole hog, and once you've tried the real thing, it's hard to go back to the shortcut version made with only pork shoulder.

For the home cook, the best strategy is to use shoulder meat along with a few ribs, a little piece of pork belly—and a pig's foot, if you can find one. Don't be too alarmed by the lard; you don't consume most of it. The lard remains in the cooking pan at the end, and any leftover pork can be submerged in the liquid fat and stored in the refrigerator for up to three days.

As for the seasonings, Fernando keeps it simple. "I'll tell you my secret," says Fernando, "nothing but garlic and whole oranges. The other secret is you add the salt at the end."

Why is that?

"Maybe if you add it at the beginning, you can oversalt the meat," Fernando speculates, although he seems not quite satisfied with his own answer.

"I don't really know," he adds after a moment. "That's the way they taught me to do it. That's what my grandfather did."

pork
IN CHILE VERDE

PORK IN *CHILE VERDE* IS ANOTHER ESSENTIAL TACO MEAT. EACH VENDOR AT GCM has a particular way of doing it, but the fundamental strategy is to stew pork for a long time in a tangy sauce of pureed tomatillos spiked with green chiles and seasoned with cilantro. In this adaption of the chile verde at Tacos Tumbras a Tomas, you first brown the pork in a small amount of lard. Vegetable oil will work, too, but lard amplifies the pork taste. Bone-in pork chops (*chuletas*) make for a more flavorful sauce, but other cuts, such as shoulder, also work well. You could even use chicken: First gently poach chicken breasts in water that has been well seasoned with salt and the juice of two lemons. Shred the meat and stew it in the salsa for 30 minutes, or until the flavors meld. This taco doesn't need a sauce, other than its owning cooking liquid. A squirt of lime juice just before serving will sharpen the flavors.

2½ pounds **bone-in pork chops** or 2 pounds **pork shoulder**, cut into 1½-inch cubes

1 teaspoon **kosher salt,** plus more as needed

1 teaspoon **lard**

1 pound **tomatillos**, hulled and quartered

1 **serrano chile** or 2 **jalapeños**, stems removed

6 to 8 fresh **cilantro** sprigs

1 **garlic clove**

1 tablespoon **vegetable oil**

Corn tortillas, store-bought or homemade (page 77), warmed

Lime wedges, for serving

1

Season the pork all over with ½ teaspoon of the salt. Melt the lard in a large skillet over high heat. Add the pork, working in batches as needed to avoid overcrowding the pan. Cook until well colored, about 5 minutes per side. Return all the pork to the pan if it's not there already, and add 1 cup water. Bring to a boil, then reduce the heat to low. Partially cover the skillet and simmer until the water has nearly evaporated, about 45 minutes, turning the meat several times during cooking.

2

Meanwhile, combine the tomatillos, serrano, and ¼ cup water in a small saucepan over medium heat. Cook for 5 minutes, or until the tomatillos soften. Transfer to a blender or food processor. Add the cilantro, garlic, and ½ teaspoon of salt and pulse until smooth. Taste and adjust the seasoning, if needed. With the motor running, stream in the vegetable oil.

3

After most of the water has evaporated in the skillet, pour the salsa over the pork. Increase the heat to high and bring the sauce to a boil, then reduce the heat to low to maintain a steady simmer and cook until the pork is very tender, another 45 minutes to 1 hour.

4

Transfer the pork to a cutting board. Pick out any bones and shred the meat. Layer the shredded meat over the corn tortillas and serve with the chile verde from the skillet spooned on top. Squeeze over some lime juice before serving.

SERVES 8

NOSE-TO-TAIL COOKING—USING EVERY PART OF THE ANIMAL, INCLUDING THE nasty bits—has been a huge trend in high-end dining for the past decade or longer. But traditional cooking from around the world also makes a virtue of frugality. The various taco vendors at GCM offer *chicharrón* (pork rind), *cabeza* (beef cheeks), *buche* (hog maw), *trompas* (snout), and *lengua* (tongue). Of all the offal, tongue is the most popular at GCM and definitely the most approachable for the squeamish. Its mild flavor and tender texture go especially well with green salsa. The standard technique is to boil the tongue, but Roast to Go poaches it in oil. The cooked tongue is then sliced thin or cut into cubes, after which you might decide to crisp the meat in a hot skillet before serving.

LENGUA
(TONGUE)
SERVES
6 TO 8

3 pounds **pork** or **cow tongue**

2 teaspoons fine **sea salt**

2 cups **vegetable oil**, plus more as needed

Green Salsa (Cooked) (page 82) or your favorite store-bought salsa, for serving

1

Preheat the oven to 325°F.

2

Scrub the tongues, and pat them dry with paper towels. Fit them snugly in a Dutch oven or a large, deep saucepan. Sprinkle with the salt, and add the oil to cover. Place the pan over medium-high heat and cook until fine bubbles start to rise from the meat, 10 to 15 minutes. Transfer the pot to the oven and cook for 1 hour for pork tongues, or 2 hours or more for cow tongue, until each is tender when pierced with a knife, turning the meat occasionally to allow for even cooking.

3

Remove the pan from the oven, and allow the meat to cool in the oil. Peel away the outer membrane and discard. Cut the meat into thin slices or chop it into small cubes. If desired, brown until crisp in a large skillet over medium-high heat. Serve with green salsa.

THIS WARM SALAD OF NOPALES, OR CACTUS PADS, IS OFTEN SERVED AS A SIDE dish, but it also works well as a vegetarian taco filling. You can skip the crumbled *queso fresco* to make it vegan, though dedicated carnivores will also appreciate nopales because their almost lemony tang cuts through meat's rich fattiness. It's like a palate cleanser between taco courses.

8 **nopales** (cactus pads), spines removed

½ bunch fresh **cilantro**

1 small **white onion**, halved

¼ teaspoon **kosher salt**

2 **Roma tomatoes**, cut into ¼-inch dice

3 **jalapeños**, seeded and diced

1 large **red onion**, diced

Corn tortillas, store-bought or homemade (page 77), warmed

2 **avocados**, sliced

¼ cup crumbled **queso fresco**

Lemon or **lime** wedges, for serving

Note: *There's no vegetable that quite matches the taste of nopales—unfortunately, if you can't find them where you live. However, you could make a tasty alternative by using green beans instead. Blanch whole trimmed green beans, slice them lengthwise ("French style"), and add extra lime or lemon juice to the dressing.*

1

Prepare the nopales: Remove any tiny, hairlike spines that might remain. Working with tongs or kitchen gloves, trim the edge off each pad, and use a sharp knife or vegetable peeler to pare off the "eyes" on each face of the pads. Cut the pads into ¼-inch strips, then cut each into ½-inch lengths.

2

Place the nopales in a medium saucepan, and cover with water. Add 3 or 4 cilantro sprigs, the halved onion, and the salt. Turn the heat to high and bring to a boil. Reduce the heat to medium and simmer for 15 minutes, or until tender, then drain.

3

In a large bowl, toss the drained nopales with the tomatoes, jalapeños, onion, and 4 or 5 springs of minced cilantro. Spoon onto corn tortillas. Garnish with the sliced avocado and crumbled queso fresco, and serve with lemon or lime wedges.

SERVES 8

NOPALES

LA TOSTADERÍA
STALL
E-10

TOSTADA
MIXTA

OWNER FERNANDO VILLAGOMEZ DESCRIBES THE OFFERINGS AT LA TOSTADERÍA AS "Sinaloan seafood," referring to the Mexican state on the country's west coast. His menu includes seafood tacos as well as a selection of ceviches—raw or blanched seafood tossed with citrus juice—served on a tostada, or a crisp whole tortilla. Fernando is a trained chef, having graduated from Le Cordon Bleu cooking school, and his recipes often include unexpected global ingredients such as fish sauce, rice vinegar, and yuzu. Even so, his tostadas come off as fairly traditional—just better. You can make this recipe without the Asian-y touches if you prefer, or adapt it to your own taste with other seasonings, vegetables, or seafood.

1 **shallot**, halved

2 **garlic cloves**, lightly crushed

2 fresh **thyme** sprigs

1 fresh **basil** sprig

3 dried **chiles de árbol**

3 tablespoons **rice vinegar**

1 teaspoon **fish sauce**

¾ teaspoon **agave syrup**

2½ teaspoons **kosher salt**, plus more as needed

1 **jalapeño**, coarsely chopped

1 **scallion** (white and green parts), coarsely chopped

1 tablespoon plus 1 teaspoon freshly squeezed **lime juice**

1 tablespoon plus 1 teaspoon freshly squeezed **orange juice**

2 tablespoons **yuzu juice** (or 1 tablespoon freshly squeezed lemon juice thinned with 1 tablespoon water)

1 pound **bay scallops**

1 pound **jumbo shrimp**, 16 to 20 count, peeled

½ pound **squid**, tubes cut into ¼-inch slices, tentacles chopped

½ medium **red bell pepper**, cut lengthwise into ¼-inch slices

1 **Persian cucumber**, cut into ½-inch dice

1 small **red onion**, thinly sliced

8 to 10 **cherry tomatoes**, halved

6 to 8 **radishes**, thinly sliced

¼ cup **cilantro leaves**

1 or 2 **habañeros**, seeded and minced

Tostadas, store-bought or homemade (page 78)

1 **avocado**, sliced, for serving

Lime wedges, for serving

Note: *Fernando insists that octopus is an essential ingredient for Tostada Mixta, but this simplified adaptation of his recipe substitutes squid, which is more widely available and easier to prepare. If you'd like to try the recipe with octopus, poach the tentacles in a seasoned bath of sake and water.*

1

Make the court bouillon: Bring 2 quarts water to a boil in a large stockpot over high heat. Add the shallot, garlic, thyme, basil, chile, 1 tablespoon of the vinegar, the fish sauce, ½ teaspoon of the agave syrup, and 2 teaspoons of the salt. Reduce the heat to low and simmer for 20 minutes. Remove the pot from the heat, and using a slotted spoon, discard the spent aromatics.

2

Meanwhile, make the vinaigrette: Combine the jalapeño, scallion, lime juice, orange juice, yuzu juice, the remaining 2 tablespoons vinegar and ¼ teaspoon agave syrup in a blender or food processor. Pulse until smooth.

3

Return the court bouillon to a boil over high heat, if it's not already. Add the scallops and poach until just translucent at the center, 1 to 2 minutes. Using a slotted spoon, transfer the scallops to a colander set over the sink. Once the liquid boils again, add the shrimp and poach until just pink, 2 to 3 minutes. Transfer to the colander. Again let the liquid return to a boil. Add the squid and poach until just heated through, 60 to 90 seconds. Transfer to the colander.

4

Transfer the cooked shellfish to a large serving bowl. Pour half the vinaigrette over them, and toss to coat. Add the bell pepper, cucumber, onion, tomatoes, radishes, whole cilantro leaves, and habañero. Toss to combine. Just before serving, season with the remaining ½ teaspoon salt. Taste and adjust the seasonings, as needed. Spoon onto tostadas to serve, garnishing each with an avocado slice and a lime wedge.

SERVES 8

CHICKEN flautas

THE SPANISH WORD *FLAUTA* MEANS "FLUTE," WHICH DESCRIBES THE SHAPE OF A tortilla tightly rolled around its filling and fried until crunchy. What makes a flauta different from a *taquito*, another fried rolled taco? There's no universal agreement, but this recipe from Roast to Go suggests one point of distinction: The flauta is made with two tortillas to create an extra-long tube. A *taquito*, which literally means "little taco," would be shorter.

1 3½-pound whole **chicken**

1 tablespoon **extra-virgin olive oil**

3 **garlic cloves**, chopped

½ teaspoon **kosher salt**

2¼ teaspoons **cumin seeds**, toasted and ground

½ cup **tomato sauce**

1 small **tomato**, seeded and chopped

1 small **yellow onion**, thinly sliced

Oil, for frying

Corn tortillas, store-bought or homemade (page 77)

OPTIONAL GARNISHES

Shredded iceberg lettuce

Chopped tomato

Minced fresh cilantro

Sour cream

Guacamole

Crumbled cotija cheese

Lime or lemon wedges

1

Rinse the chicken and pat it dry. Coat it all over with the olive oil, and rub it with two-thirds of the chopped garlic, the salt, and ¼ teaspoon of the ground cumin. Place it in a roasting pan and let it sit at room temperature for 30 minutes.

2

Preheat the oven to 400°F. Transfer the baking sheet to the oven and roast the chicken for 15 minutes, then reduce the heat to 350°F and bake until it's golden brown and the leg joint is loose when you wiggle it, 45 minutes to 1 hour more. Remove the chicken from the oven and let it cool for 15 minutes. Using tongs or your fingers, shred the meat into bite-size pieces, discarding the bones and skin.

3

In a large saucepan over high heat, combine the tomato sauce, chopped tomato, onion, remaining garlic, remaining 2 teaspoons ground cumin, and 1 cup water. Bring to a boil, then add the shredded chicken. Reduce the heat to medium and cook for 15 minutes, or until the chicken has absorbed the seasoning. Remove the pan from the heat, and let cool.

4

Heat 2 inches of oil in a deep cast-iron skillet or Dutch oven over high heat to 350°F. Quickly add the tortillas, one at a time, just to soften, a second or two per side. Drain on a paper-towel-lined tray. Remove the skillet with the oil from the heat, reserving it.

5

To assemble, lay 2 tortillas on a flat surface so that they overlap a bit, like the MasterCard logo or a Venn diagram. Pick up about 3 tablespoons of filling with your hand and squeeze out the excess liquid. Place the filling in the middle of the tortillas, and roll them into a tube. Secure with two toothpicks.

6

Reheat the oil to 350°F. Add the flautas, a few at a time, and fry for 2 minutes, or until crisp and golden. Drain on a paper-towel-lined tray. Serve with the garnishes of your choice.

SERVES 8 TO 10

DURING THE EATING OUT LOUD EVENT WITH *LUCKY PEACH* IN **2016** (SEE OPPOSITE for more about that), taco fans ran straight for Chiles Secos, where Claudia Armendariz, granddaughter of Chiles Secos founder Celestino López, teamed up with Carlos Salgado, the chef at Taco Maria in Orange County. Salgado cooks in a style that's sometimes called Alta California cuisine, which updates historical Mexican cuisine and pre-Columbian cooking. Claudia and Carlos took two ancient ingredients, corn and duck, and modernized them with dates. The rich, spicy, and slightly sweet mole splashed over the top was originally another kind of collaboration. Various legends tell that mole was invented around Puebla, Mexico, in the sixteenth century. The historical fact is that it combined New World ingredients— ground seeds, dried fruit, a touch of chocolate—with Old World spices to create something new. It's the original New World fusion.

DUCK FLAUTAS
WITH DATES & MOLE AJONJOLI

6 **duck legs** (drumstick and thigh together)

Kosher salt and freshly ground **black pepper**

Leaves only from 5 or 6 fresh **thyme** sprigs

½ cup **duck fat** or **extra-virgin olive oil**

¼ cup **mole ajonjoli** (see Notes)

1 cup **chicken stock** or **water**

20 **flour tortillas**, store-bought or homemade (page 77), warmed

10 fresh **dates**, pitted and halved lengthwise

Oil, for frying

2 tablespoons toasted **sesame seeds**

Notes: Mole ajonjoli (*sesame-seed mole*) *is sold at Chiles Secos and other Latin markets. Mole poblano works well, too.*

The duck legs need to marinate overnight before cooking.

1

Season the duck legs generously with salt, pepper, and the thyme leaves. Arrange them in a single layer on a baking sheet, and cover with plastic wrap. Refrigerate overnight.

2

The next day, preheat the oven to 225°F. Melt the duck fat in a small saucepan over low heat, and brush it over the marinated duck legs. Transfer the baking sheet to the oven and roast for 3 hours, or until the skin is crisp and the drumstick moves freely when you wiggle it. Remove and set aside to cool for 15 minutes, then using tongs or your fingers, pick the meat, discarding the bones.

3

Meanwhile, make the mole sauce: Melt the mole paste in a small saucepan over medium heat. When it sizzles, whisk in ¼ cup of the stock. Bring to a boil and cook until thick before adding another ¼ cup of the stock. Repeat in ¼-cup increments until all the liquid is incorporated, then simmer until the sauce has the consistency of a milk shake. Remove the pan from the heat and cover to keep warm.

4

Assemble the flautas: Lay out one warm tortilla on a dry surface, and spread about 2 tablespoons of the filling down the middle. Place half a date on top. Roll up the tortilla and secure with a toothpick. Repeat with the remaining tortillas and filling.

5

Heat 2 inches of oil in a deep cast-iron skillet or Dutch oven to 350°F. Add the flautas, a few at a time, and fry for 2 minutes, or until crispy and golden. Drain on a paper-towel-lined tray. Transfer to a serving platter, and spoon the mole over the top. Garnish with sesame seeds.

SERVES 8 TO 10

IN THE DEAD OF WINTER IN 2016, *LUCKY PEACH* magazine ditched snowy New York and came to Los Angeles for the first time to present Eating Out Loud, a live event of readings and performances by chefs David Chang and Roy Choi, food critic Jonathan Gold, Sonic Youth's Kim Gordon, and actor Eric Wareheim. The performances took place at the Million Dollar Theatre, next door to GCM, and afterward everyone spilled into the Market for a party. *Lucky Peach* had invited a few outside chefs to collaborate with Market vendors, so for one night the GCM lineup included Madcapra + Brooks Headley of Superiority Burger, DTLA Cheese + Jessica Koslow of Sqirl, and Wexler's Deli + Jon Shook and Vinny Dotolo of Animal. Lines snaked down the aisles.

CHIVO

(STEWED GOAT)

ONE ITEM STILL ON THE MENU AT ROAST TO GO, MORE THAN SIXTY YEARS AFTER this oldest vendor arrived at the Market, is *chivo*, or goat. The taste is pleasantly distinctive, not gamey. If you tasted it blind, you would probably guess it wasn't beef but couldn't say why. Belcampo Meat Company sells goat meat at its GCM butcher counter, and the meat has enjoyed some popularity among foodies for its novelty, and because it is a more environmentally sustainable red meat than beef. Goat stands up well to long, slow cooking and strong flavors. In this recipe, the cooked meat is shredded and served on tacos with fiery Red Salsa (page 82). Then the cooking broth is strained to serve as a consommé—either alongside the tacos or as separate course. Garnish the soup with a little chopped onion, cilantro, and a pinch of shredded meat.

4 pounds **goat meat**, cut into 2-inch chunks

1 small **onion**, halved

1 small head of **garlic**, cut in half crosswise

2 teaspoons fine **sea salt**, plus more as needed

4 whole **bay leaves**

2 tablespoons **dried oregano**

2 tablespoons **cumin seeds**

Corn tortillas, store-bought or homemade (page 77), for serving

Red Salsa (page 82), or your favorite store-bought salsa, for serving

Note: *The cooked goat should be chilled overnight in the refrigerator so that the rendered fat hardens, making it easy to degrease the cooking broth.*

1

Combine the meat, onion, and garlic in large pot, then add 4 quarts water. Bring to a boil over high heat, then reduce the heat to medium-low to maintain a steady simmer. After 30 minutes, skim the surface. Add the salt, bay leaves, oregano, and cumin seeds. Cook for 3½ hours more. Taste and adjust the seasonings, if needed. Remove the pot from the heat, and allow it to cool for 15 minutes. Cover the pot and refrigerate overnight.

2

The next day, skim the fat off the surface of the broth and discard. Gently rewarm the pot over low heat for 20 minutes, or until the meat is heated through. Lift out the meat with a slotted spoon, reserving the broth in the pot. Using tongs or your fingers, shred the meat, discarding the bones. Place 2 to 3 tablespoons of meat on top of each tortilla, and finish with salsa.

3

Strain the reserved broth through a fine-mesh sieve. Serve in cups alongside the tacos or as a separate course. Store the consommé in an airtight container in the refrigerator for up to 3 days.

SERVES 8 TO 10

AL PASTOR (SEASONED PORK)

TACOS AL PASTOR ARE A PRIME EXAMPLE OF HOW MEXICAN CUISINE HAS absorbed and adapted foreign influences. Literally meaning "shepherd's style," al pastor was inspired by shawarma-style grilled, marinated meat brought to Mexico by Lebanese immigrants. Something was gained in translation. The traditional Lebanese lamb was replaced with pork, and the Mexican marinade picked up the New World flavors of pineapple, chiles, and achiote paste, a highly flavored mix of annatto seeds, spices, and garlic that stains the meat red. Al pastor tacos don't necessarily need a flavor boost from salsa, but if you want an added kick, the fiery, fruity heat of Habañero Salsa (page 82) pairs particularly well.

6 dried **guajillo chiles**

2 dried **pasilla chiles**

½ fresh **pineapple**, quartered, peeled, cored, and cut into ½-inch slices (about 6 cups)

6 **garlic cloves**

1 teaspoon **kosher salt**

¼ teaspoon freshly ground **black pepper**

2 tablespoons **achiote paste**, store-bought or homemade (recipe opposite)

3 pounds **bone-in pork chops**, ½-inch thick

1 tablespoon **vegetable oil**

1 teaspoon **sugar**

Corn tortillas, store-bought or homemade (page 77), warmed

Note: *The meat will need to marinate for at least an hour, and preferably overnight. The bone-in pork chops called for could be replaced by other cuts, such as loin chops or steaks cut from the pork shoulder.*

1

In a large dry skillet over medium heat, toast the chiles until flexible and fragrant, 10 seconds per side. Remove from the heat to cool for a few seconds, then remove the stems, veins, and seeds. Transfer the chiles to a small saucepan and add water to cover them halfway. Cover the pot, and cook over medium heat until the chiles are soft, 10 to 15 minutes. Reserve 1 cup of the cooking water, then drain the chiles.

2

In a blender or food processor, combine the chiles, 1 cup reserved cooking liquid, 4 cups of the pineapple, the garlic, salt, black pepper, and achiote paste. Pulse until smooth. Place the pork chops in a large bowl and pour the puree over them. Cover and marinate in the refrigerator for at least 2 hours, preferably overnight. Remove from the refrigerator 1 hour before cooking.

3

Preheat the grill or broiler. Remove the pork chops from the marinade, wiping off any excess. Grill them over medium heat until lightly charred and cooked through, 6 to 8 minutes per side. Alternatively, arrange the chops on a baking sheet and broil them for 6 to 8 minutes per side. Transfer the pork chops to a tray to rest for 10 minutes, leaving the grill or broiler on.

4

Meanwhile, toss the remaining 2 cups pineapple slices in a large bowl with the oil and sugar. Grill or broil them until lightly caramelized, 2 to 3 minutes per side. Remove from the heat.

5

Cut the pork chops into thin slices, discarding the bones and reserving any juices from the tray. Toss the sliced pork with the reserved juices. To serve, spoon the pork over warm tortillas and serve a slice of grilled pineapple alongside.

SERVES 8

ACHIOTE PASTE

½ teaspoon **cumin seeds**

½ teaspoon **coriander seeds**

1 whole **clove**

1 tablespoon **achiote** powder

¼ teaspoon freshly ground **black pepper**

½ teaspoon dried **Mexican oregano**

½ teaspoon **kosher salt**

4 **garlic cloves**, minced

1 tablespoon **rice vinegar**

Zest from ½ **orange**

Toast the cumin, coriander, and clove together in a small dry skillet until fragrant, 1 to 2 minutes. Transfer to a mortar, spice mill, or food processor, and grind as finely as possible. Add the achiote, pepper, oregano, and salt. Grind to incorporate. Transfer to a small bowl, and add the garlic, vinegar, and zest. Mix to incorporate into a thick paste.

MAKES 3 TABLESPOONS

VEGAN
CRUNCHY
AVOCADO
TACOS

WITH CORN SALSA
& CHIPOTLE "MAYO"

IF YOU THINK ABOUT IT, MOST OF THE WORLD'S GREAT DRINKING FOOD IS MEAT based. Why? Because crunchy, rich, salty, fatty, spicy food tastes great with beer, and it provides enough ballast to keep you from falling off the barstool. But all of that also holds true for this new-wave taco from Golden Road Brewing, which is made from panko-crusted avocados splashed with smoky chipotle. Golden Road cofounder Tony Yanow is vegan, so he wanted to offer a menu that would both fit the spirit of Grand Central Market's taco culture and also provide options for plant-based eaters like him.

2 cups **vegan mayonnaise**, preferably Vegenaise

2 tablespoons minced canned **chipotles in adobo**

Juice of 1 **lemon**

Kosher salt and freshly ground **black pepper**

1½ cups all-purpose **flour**, plus more as needed

½ teaspoon **garlic powder**

½ teaspoon **chili powder**

1 cup **lager beer**, plus more as needed

3 large **avocados** (not too ripe)

2 cups **panko bread crumbs**

Oil, for frying

18 **corn tortillas,** store-bought or homemade (page 77), warmed

GARNISHES

Shredded red cabbage

Corn Salsa (page 85)

Lime wedges

1
In a small bowl, whisk together the vegan mayo, chipotles, and lemon juice until smooth. Season with salt and pepper to taste.

2
Stir together the flour, garlic powder, and chili powder in a large bowl. Add the beer and whisk until smooth. The mixture should have the consistency of pancake batter; add more beer or flour to adjust, as needed.

3
Working with one at a time, cut an unpeeled avocado lengthwise into 6 pieces. Loosen the wedges with the edge of your knife, and remove the peel. Dip each slice of avocado into the batter, allowing any excess to drip off, then roll it through the panko, pressing it to adhere. Place the coated slices on a tray.

4
Heat 2 inches of oil in a Dutch oven to 375°F. Working in small batches, fry the avocados until they are golden brown, about 3 minutes. Transfer to a paper-towel-lined tray to drain.

5
To assemble, lay out a tortilla on the counter. Start with a layer of cabbage, then a slice of fried avocado. Top with dollops of the chipotle "mayo" and corn salsa. Serve with lime wedges.

SERVES 6 TO 8

SARAH CLARK, THE CHEF BEHIND SARITA'S PUPUSERIA, BUILT HER BUSINESS BY adapting the traditional *pupusa*—a stuffed, griddled masa cake from her home country, El Salvador—to suit Angeleno tastes. In particular, she spotlighted vegetable pupusas filled with broccoli and spinach, which is a good tip-off that the basic pupusa technique described in this recipe is easy and adaptable to many different fillings and flavors. You could replace the spinach with kale, for instance, or very thinly sliced rounds of zucchini. Or you could dream up entirely new—and entirely untraditional—fillings, such as roasted red peppers with feta, or grilled eggplant with mozzarella, or a handful of chopped herbs with goat cheese. Another bestseller at Sarita's swaps out the spinach for ¼ pound of raw, chopped shrimp. *Curdito,* a tangy, spicy slaw, is the standard side dish with any pupusa.

The skill and artistry of pupusas lies in wrapping a generous filling within an evenly thin, supple masa envelope. If the masa is too thick, especially around the edges, the dough won't cook all the way through. Too thin, and the filling spills out. It takes practice to get right, but masa is inexpensive, and even the mistakes taste good.

SPINACH & CHEESE
pupusas
WITH CURTIDO

2 cups **masa harina**

1 cup packed coarsely chopped **spinach**

1 cup grated **Monterey Jack cheese**

Hot sauce and **Curtido** (recipe follows), for serving

1

Place the masa in a large bowl, and pour in 2 cups warm water. Stir together with your hand. Lightly knead the dough in the bowl until it becomes less sticky as the masa absorbs the water. The consistency should be firm but pliable, like cookie dough. If it's too dry, add a bit more water; if it's too wet, add a bit more masa. Shape the dough into a ball, and cover the bowl with a kitchen towel. Set aside to rest for 10 minutes.

2

Heat a comal, griddle, or cast-iron skillet over medium heat. Divide the masa evenly into 4 portions. Working with one at a time, form the masa into a ball. Hollow out the ball with your thumb to make a thick-walled "indentation," taking care not to go all the way through the other side. Take a quarter of the spinach, and press it into a ball with a quarter of the cheese. Stuff the filling into the cup in the masa, and wrap the dough around the filling until it's completely enclosed. Place it on a flat surface, and gently flatten the dough with your palm until it's about 5 inches across and less than ½ inch thick.

3

Put the pupusa in the hot skillet, and cook until golden and toasted in spots, 6 to 8 minutes per side. Serve with hot sauce and curtido.

MAKES 4 PUPUSAS

RECIPE CONTINUES

CURTIDO

½ medium head **green cabbage**, finely shredded

1 large **carrot**, grated

½ medium **yellow onion**, thinly sliced

½ teaspoon **kosher salt**

1 teaspoon dried **oregano**

½ teaspoon dried **red chile flakes**, or to taste

A few pinches of **sugar**

¼ to ⅓ cup **apple cider vinegar**

Combine the shredded cabbage, carrot, and onion in a large bowl, and sprinkle with the salt. Knead the vegetables together to soften them slightly. Season with oregano, chile flakes, sugar, and ¼ cup of the vinegar. Taste, and adjust the seasonings to your liking. Set aside to marinate at room temperature for at least a couple of hours before using. Store in the refrigerator covered—the curtido will be even better the next day.

MAKES 3 CUPS

CARBS

PAD KEE MAO

KEE MAO

(DRUNKEN NOODLES)

THE NAME "DRUNKEN NOODLES" MISLEADS: IT'S NOT THE NOODLES THAT ARE full of booze, but the person eating them. At least that's one theory behind this classic Thai stir-fry. Some say *pad kee mao* was invented as a midnight snack to cap off a bar crawl; others say it was meant as a morning-after cure. Either way, a plate of rice noodles coated with brown sauce and studded with chunks of sautéed chicken and crunchy vegetables is pure Thai comfort food. Drunken Noodles go well with any hour of the day or night, although a bottle of beer helps cool down the spicy heat.

This recipe from Sticky Rice II sticks with tradition. There's an influence of Chinese cooking, even though the flavor profile from fresh chiles and whole basil leaves is distinctly Thai. Everything needs to be cooked quickly over very high heat. In fact, you might even consider dividing your ingredients in step 2 below and sautéing the chicken, vegetables, and noodles in two batches.

½ pound skinless, boneless **chicken breast**

Juice of 1 **lemon**

½ teaspoon **kosher salt**

2 tablespoons **vegetable oil**

¾ cup sliced **yellow onions**

¾ cup thinly sliced **carrots**

¾ cup thinly sliced **red bell peppers**

¾ cup sliced button **mushrooms**

2 **serrano chiles**, seeded and sliced

3 tablespoons minced **garlic** (about 6 cloves)

1 pound wide, flat **rice noodles**, prepared according to package instructions

3 tablespoons **oyster sauce**

3 tablespoons **sweet soy sauce** (see page 116)

3 tablespoon **sambal oelek chili paste**

¼ cup **Thai basil** leaves, tightly packed

1

Place the chicken breast, lemon juice, and salt in a small saucepan and cover with water by 1 inch. Bring to a boil over medium heat, then reduce the heat to low and simmer until the chicken is cooked through and no longer pink, 12 to 15 minutes. Drain the chicken and let cool for 5 minutes, then cut into ¼-inch slices.

2

Heat the oil in a large sauté pan over high heat. When the oil is smoking, add the sliced chicken, onion, carrots, bell peppers, mushrooms, serranos, and half the garlic. Sauté until the onion is translucent and the mushrooms are softened, about 5 minutes. Add the cooked noodles, oyster sauce, sweet soy sauce, and sambal oelek, and toss to combine. Continue cooking until the liquid is reduced, about 3 minutes. Add the remaining garlic and sauté for 30 seconds more until fragrant.

3

To serve, add the Thai basil and toss to combine.

SERVES 4

KUAY tiao REUA
(BOAT NOODLES)

STICKY RICE II IS OWNER DAVID TEWASART'S TRIBUTE TO NOODLES, AND THE menu covers the two major categories of noodles in Thai cuisine: stir-fried and soup. Among the latter, Boat Noodles steal the show, thanks to the dish's subtle beef broth seasoned with ginger, garlic, cilantro, and fish sauce—standard elements of the Thai flavor palette. Spices such as star anise and clove add beguiling extra layers of fragrance. The sweet-savory taste builds with sweet soy sauce, which has a molasses-y color and taste thanks to palm sugar. (Sweet soy sauce is widely available.) The goal in seasoning the broth is to balance the sweet elements against the salty-funky umami taste of fish sauce, with the sweet being ever so slightly in the lead. You can also add extra vegetables or meat, such as the Thai meatballs shown opposite

4 quarts **beef stock**

2 pounds **brisket**

2 medium **yellow onions**, unpeeled and halved

2 **cilantro roots** (or 4 to 6 fresh cilantro sprigs)

1 3-inch piece **fresh ginger**, peeled and halved lengthwise

10 **garlic cloves**

3 whole **star anise**

1 tablespoon whole **cloves**

1 tablespoon **black peppercorns**

1 tablespoon **white peppercorns**

1 tablespoon **coriander seeds**

3 tablespoons **fish sauce**, plus more as needed

¼ cup **sweet soy sauce**, plus more as needed

1 tablespoon **light soy sauce**

1 tablespoon **palm sugar** or **turbinado sugar**

Kosher salt

2 cups **bean sprouts**

1 pound **Chinese broccoli** or **bok choy**, cut into 1-inch pieces

1 pound thin **rice noodles**, cooked according to package directions

½ cup **celery leaves**, chopped

½ cup **cilantro** leaves, chopped

Dried **red chile flakes** (optional)

Note: *The soup's base of brisket gently poached in beef stock will take about 2 hours on the stove, but the pot can take care of itself as it simmers. After that, the rest of the preparation comes together quickly.*

1

Combine the stock, brisket, onions, cilantro root, ginger, garlic, star anise, cloves, black pepper, white pepper, and coriander in a large stockpot and bring to a boil over high heat. Reduce the heat to low, and simmer until the brisket is fork-tender, about 2 hours. Remove the pot from the heat. Transfer the brisket to a platter, and cover with aluminum foil to keep warm.

2

Strain the broth through a fine-mesh sieve set over a large bowl; discard the solids. Return the broth to the stockpot. Add the fish sauce, sweet soy sauce, light soy sauce, and sugar. Taste and adjust the balance of the fish sauce and sweet soy sauce, if needed, so that the broth tastes slightly more sweet than salty.

3

Meanwhile, bring a separate large pot of well-salted water to a boil over high heat. Add the bean sprouts and blanch until tender, about 1 minute. Using a spider or slotted spoon, transfer the sprouts to a medium bowl, reserving the cooking water in the pot and keeping the heat on. Add the Chinese broccoli to the pot, and blanch until just tender, 2 to 3 minutes. Transfer to the bowl with the bean sprouts.

4

Cut the brisket into ¼-inch slices. Reheat the broth over high heat until it boils. To serve, divide the cooked rice noodles among bowls. Divide the Chinese broccoli, bean sprouts, and sliced brisket among the bowls. Cover with the broth. Garnish with celery leaves, cilantro leaves, and chile flakes, if desired.

IN **2017**, THE BEST PLACE TO TASTE TRADITIONAL CHINESE COOKING IN LOS Angeles is not historic Chinatown, just north of Grand Central Market, but out in the suburbs of the San Gabriel Valley. The best place for "SoCal Chinese," on the other hand, is GCM's China Cafe, which has been serving up an Americanized version of Chinese-diaspora cooking since 1959 (see page 120 for more about that). Generations of Market visitors have found China Cafe's version of chow mein comforting, familiar, and delicious. It is a homey dish of stir-fried yellow egg noodles with crisp broccoli and bean sprouts seasoned with oyster sauce. The recipe can be adapted to include whatever vegetables you like, as well as chunks of sautéed chicken, a handful of shrimp, or slices of roast pork.

1 cup **broccoli** florets

½ pound **bok choy**, sliced into 1-inch pieces

2 tablespoons **vegetable oil**

1 pound thin **Chinese egg noodles**, cooked according to package instructions

½ teaspoon **sugar**

1 teaspoon **chicken bouillon powder**, preferably Knorr

2 teaspoons **mushroom soy sauce** (or other Chinese dark soy sauce)

2 teaspoons **oyster sauce**

2 cups **bean sprouts**

2 **scallions** (white and green parts), cut into 1-inch lengths

1

Bring a medium pot of water to a boil over high heat. Add the broccoli florets and blanch for 1 minute, until they turn bright green, then add the bok choy. Blanch for 2 minutes more, or until the vegetables are just tender. Drain and set aside.

2

Heat the oil in a wok or large sauté pan over high heat. When the oil shimmers, add the cooked noodles, sugar, and bouillon. Sauté for 1 minute, until the noodles are coated. Add the soy sauce and oyster sauce, and continue cooking until the liquids reduce, about 2 minutes more. Taste and adjust the seasoning, if needed.

3

Add the blanched bok choy and broccoli to the wok, and toss to combine. Add the bean sprouts and scallions, and sauté until the bean sprouts are heated through, 1 to 2 minutes. Serve immediately.

VEGETABLE *chow* MEIN

SERVES 4

CHINA CAFE'S MENU presents an interesting question. Does it serve Chinese food? Well, yes and no. What it serves is Southern California Chinese food. Chow mein and chop suey aren't traditional dishes from China, but were invented in America a hundred years ago by Chinese-born chefs using local ingredients to please a nonimmigrant clientele. And since GCM's founding in 1917, this style of "Chinese food" has been a draw. A 1922 advertising brochure promoted the Cherry Blossom, a Chinese restaurant in the basement.

A closer look at the plates on China Cafe's counters shows how SoCal Chinese cooking is continuing to evolve. A lot of the customers at China Cafe are Latino, and you often see them customize their orders with hot sauce and limes. Others add an avocado or jalapeño they picked up at one of GCM's produce stalls. The result is spontaneous culinary fusion—though most chefs hate that term these days.

Still, whatever you call it, China Cafe provides an example of how food traditions adapt to local circumstances. Chefs at high-end restaurants around Los Angeles are also creating high-end mash-ups of Asian, Latin, and Anglo-European influences. This style of transcultural invention isn't "authentic" to any single background culture; it's more like a vision of the *Blade Runner* future beamed into the here and now. At GCM, we call it the "new authentic," a new way of cooking that reflects the reality of twenty-first-century America's culinary diversity.

CURRY
UDON

UDON ARE PENCIL-THICK JAPANESE WHEAT NOODLES TYPICALLY SERVED IN A large bowl with broth—hot in the winter, cold in the summer. The noodles themselves are pleasantly chewy but bland, so they benefit from strong flavors. Bento Ya dunks its udon in a warming broth that's thick with curry paste and bobbing with bits of chicken and hunks of potato. A bowl of Curry Udon is a full meal, but you could also round out the table with tempura vegetables, *tonkatsu* (deep fried pork cutlet), or even a California roll.

2 tablespoons **vegetable oil**

1 medium **yellow onion**, chopped

½ teaspoon ground **cumin**

2 teaspoons ground **turmeric**

½ teaspoon **chili powder**

1 teaspoon sweet **paprika**

½ pound boneless, skinless **chicken thighs**, cut into ½-inch pieces

2 **carrots**, cut into ¼-inch rounds

5 cups **chicken stock**

2 **Yukon Gold potatoes**, peeled and cut into ¼-inch cubes

1 tablespoon **all-purpose flour**

1 tablespoon **cornstarch**

1 pound **udon noodles**, prepared according to package instructions

1 **scallion** (white and green parts), chopped

1

Heat the oil in a large sauté pan over high heat. When the oil shimmers, add the onion and cook until it begins to color, 5 to 7 minutes. Add the cumin, turmeric, chili powder, and paprika, and toss to coat, then add the chicken and carrots. Sauté until the chicken is just opaque, about 3 minutes. Add the stock and the potatoes. Bring to a boil, then reduce the heat to medium and simmer until the chicken is cooked through and the potatoes are tender, 8 to 10 minutes.

2

In a small bowl, whisk together ¼ cup water, the flour, and the cornstarch. Add the mixture to the pan. Increase the heat to high, return to a boil, and cook until the sauce thickens slightly, 2 to 3 minutes. Add the cooked udon, and toss to coat. Garnish with the chopped scallion and serve.

SERVES 4

AS WITH MANY NOODLE RECIPES, Bento Ya's recipe for Curry Udon can be adapted in any way you like—replacing chicken with shrimp, for instance, or adding a handful of chopped vegetables. Culinary history proves the point. Udon trace their origin to China, where the first noodles likely appeared over two thousand years ago. Noodles eventually made their way throughout Asia and around the world. Along the way, the original Chinese concept evolved into everything from Japanese udon and ramen to Thai rice noodles to Italian spaghetti and fettucine.

Curry has traveled almost as far in a much shorter time. It arrived in Japan from the Indian subcontinent about 150 years ago, but Japanese chefs decided to turn down the fire and spice to suit the nuances of Japanese cuisine.

Tasty history lesson aside, the point is that food travels with people and has since the beginning of time. It's a natural corollary that people have always adapt cuisines to accommodate local taste. A recipe like Curry Udon isn't written in stone; It's an invitation to change.

RAHUL KHOPKAR'S vegan broth for Cold Smoky Ramen is a sleight of hand—where's the meat?—that relies on a couple of tricks of food science. The first is umami, the meaty deliciousness provided here by dried shiitake mushrooms and kombu (dried kelp). Next is caramelization and the Maillard reaction, both chemical processes that develop color and flavor in the onions as they brown slowly over low heat. The third is smoke. At Ramen Hood, Rahul cold-smokes the onions before caramelizing them, but more practical for the home cook is using smoked salt to season the finished broth. Smoked salt is widely available in supermarket spice aisles or can be ordered online from Jacobsen Salt Company. The entire process does take time and planning—to soak the shiitake and kombu, and to chill the broth—but is not complicated. In return you get a dozen servings of delicious cold noodles—enough to get you and your friends through the next big heat wave.

FAIR WARNING: THIS RECIPE IS A PROJECT. BUT WHEN THE TEMPERATURE IN
DTLA soars past 90—which could happen any month of the year and does ever more often these days—there's no better lunch than a bowl of cold ramen at Ramen Hood. The broth is deep and soulful, but transparently light. As a result, the unique texture and flavor of the buckwheat noodles becomes an important element of the dish—not just a bland carb filler. The twist is that chef Rahul Khopkar's ramen broth, adapted here for home use, is totally vegan. (The sidebar opposite shares his tricks.)

cold SMOKY RAMEN

SERVES 12

½ cup dried **shiitake mushrooms**

1 2 × 4-inch piece **kombu** (optional)

2 tablespoons **vegetable oil**

2 pounds large **yellow onions**, thinly sliced

1½ teaspoons **kosher salt**, plus more for blanching

3 large **portobello mushrooms**, cut into ½-inch slices

3 tablespoons **smoked salt** (see sidebar)

2 tablespoons **extra-virgin olive oil**

2 teaspoons **nutritional yeast**

2 pounds **baby bok choy**, quartered

3 tablespoons **toasted sesame oil**

¾ pound **bean spouts**

2 pounds **soba noodles**, prepared according to package instructions

¼ teaspoon **chili oil**

4 **scallions** (white and green parts), chopped

Dried **red chile flakes** and toasted **sesame seeds**, for garnish

Note: *Even if you're not up for the entire recipe, consider making a batch of roasted portobello mushrooms seasoned with nutritional yeast, as described in step 4. Nutritional yeast is available in the health-food aisle. Using it to season portobellos is a brilliant and easy technique that creates a roasted mushroom savory enough to anchor a meat-free sandwich or any vegetarian feast.*

1

Place the dried shiitake and kombu, if using, in a medium bowl. Cover with 4 cups water, and let steep at room temperature for at least 1 hour, or up to overnight.

2

Heat the vegetable oil in a large stockpot over medium heat. When the oil shimmers, add the onions and 1 teaspoon of the kosher salt. Sauté until the onions are medium brown, 25 to 30 minutes. Add the shiitake, kombu, steeping water, ½ cup of the sliced portobellos, and 4 quarts more water. Increase the heat to high and bring to a boil, then reduce the heat to medium and simmer for 30 minutes.

RECIPE CONTINUES

Remove the pot from the heat and allow it to cool at room temperature for 30 minutes.

3

Strain the broth through a fine-mesh sieve placed over a large container; discard the solids. You will have about 4 quarts of broth. Stir in 2 tablespoons of the smoked salt. Let cool to room temperature before covering. Store in the refrigerator overnight.

4

Meanwhile, preheat the oven to 450°F. Arrange the remaining portobellos on a baking sheet. Drizzle 1 tablespoon of the olive oil over them, and sprinkle with ¼ teaspoon of the kosher salt and 1 teaspoon of the nutritional yeast. Flip over the mushrooms and repeat on the other side. Transfer to the oven and roast for 15 minutes. Remove and let cool. Transfer to an airtight container and refrigerate overnight.

5

An hour before serving, boil a large pot of well-salted water over high heat. Fill a large bowl with ice and water. Add the baby bok choy to the boiling water and blanch for 2 to 3 minutes, until just tender. Using a slotted spoon, transfer them to the ice bath, reserving the blanching water in the pot. Drain the bok choy, and transfer them to a medium bowl. Add 2 tablespoons of the sesame oil and toss to coat. Add the bean sprouts to the pot of boiling water and blanch for 1 minute, until just tender. Transfer to the ice bath, then drain and toss them in a medium bowl with the remaining 1 tablespoon sesame oil.

6

Remove the broth and roasted portobellos from the refrigerator.

Taste the broth and adjust the seasoning with the remaining smoked salt, if needed.

7

To serve, ladle 1½ cups of broth into a large soup bowl. Add about 1⅓ cups chilled soba and a few drops of chili oil. Using chopsticks or a spoon, gently move the soba noodles around to unstick them. Add the bean sprouts and bok choy. Top with a slice of roasted portobello and garnish with chile flakes and sesame seeds.

LINGUINE
WITH LAMB SAUSAGE & MOLE

AT FIRST GLANCE, THIS ITALIAN PASTA SAUCED WITH MEXICAN MOLE SEEMS
plain weird. But in the kitchen, the elements come together in a way that seems almost predestined. Claudia Armendariz of Chiles Secos recalls her first time making this dish as a spur-of-the-moment inspiration. She was staring at the jumbled ingredients in her fridge and wondering what in the world to do with them when lightning struck.

The mole poblano—a complex blend of chiles, spices, and a very small amount of Mexican chocolate—forms a rich sauce that coats the linguine and ties together the crumbled lamb sausage, lightly sautéed squash, and blanched green beans. The salty tang of sheep's-milk ricotta salata and the crisp fried sage leaves work as a counterpoint to the mole's subtle heat and creamy smoothness. All in all, it's a masterful combination of flavors—and a perfect illustration of how new Los Angeles cooking transcends geographic boundaries and culinary stereotypes.

⅓ cup **mole poblano paste** (see page 45)

½ cup **heavy cream**

½ teaspoon **kosher salt**, plus more for the pot

¾ pound **green beans**, trimmed

2 tablespoons **vegetable oil**

20 fresh **sage** leaves

2 **garlic cloves**, lightly crushed

¾ pound **yellow squash**, cut into ¼-inch slices

1 pound **lamb sausages**, removed from their casings

1 pound **linguine**, prepared according to package instructions and kept warm

½ cup crumbled **ricotta salata**

Note: *Save yourself a pot to wash: After you blanch the beans, lift them out with a spider or slotted spoon. Reserve the water, and return it to a boil when you're ready to cook the pasta.*

1
Melt the mole in a small saucepan over medium heat. Whisk in 1 cup water, ¼ cup at a time, incorporating each addition before adding the next. Bring to a boil, and cook for 3 minutes, or until the mole coats the back of a spoon. Whisk in the cream. Reduce the heat to low and cover the pot to keep the mole warm.

2
Bring a large pot of salted water to a boil over high heat. Add the beans and blanch until just tender, 2 to 3 minutes. Using a slotted spoon, transfer the beans to a large serving bowl.

3
Heat the oil in a large sauté pan over medium heat. When the oil shimmers, add the sage and fry until crisp, about 1 minute. Transfer to a paper-towel-lined plate to drain. Add the garlic to the pan and cook until golden, about 1 minute. Add the squash and ¼ teaspoon salt. Sauté until tender, 8 to 10 minutes. Season with ¼ teaspoon salt. Transfer to the bowl with the beans.

4
In the same sauté pan, cook the sausage over medium heat until browned, 7 to 9 minutes. Pour off the excess fat. Transfer the sausage to the bowl with the vegetables. Add the cooked linguine and the ricotta salata. Pour the mole over and toss to combine. Garnish with the fried sage leaves.

SERVES 4 TO 6

SPAGHETTI

WITH

SUNDAY

GRAVY

"GRAVY" IS CHEF BRUCE KALMAN'S VERSION OF A CLASSIC ITALIAN-STYLE RED sauce, and he modifies that with "Sunday" because it's the kind of big dish—big flavors, big portions—that will satisfy everyone at a large family gathering. Bruce's sauce combines various cuts of flavorful meat simmered for hours with San Marzano tomatoes, fresh herbs, and pungent aromatics. Even in carb-phobic Los Angeles, it's a bestseller.

2 tablespoons **extra-virgin olive oil**

1 fresh **oregano** sprig

3 fresh **basil** sprigs, tied in bundle

½ pound **pork shoulder**

½ pound **beef chuck**

½ pound **beef shank**, cut into 2-inch pieces

Kosher salt and freshly ground **black pepper**

¼ teaspoon dried **red chile flakes**

3 **garlic cloves**, crushed

1 small **yellow onion**, diced

¾ cup **dry red wine**

2 28-ounce cans whole **San Marzano tomatoes**

3 pounds **spaghetti**, prepared according to package instructions, for serving

1 cup grated **Parmesan cheese**, for serving

1

Preheat the oven to 300°F.

2

Heat the oil in a large Dutch oven over medium heat. When the oil shimmers, add the oregano and basil, and fry until crisp, about 1 minute per side. Transfer the herbs to a paper-towel-lined plate to drain, reserving the oil in the pot.

3

Season the meats generously with salt and black pepper. Increase the heat under the Dutch oven to high. Working in batches, add the meat and cook until deeply browned, 6 to 8 minutes per side. Transfer the meat to a tray. Add the chile flakes, garlic, and onion to the pot, and season with salt and black pepper. Sauté until the onion is translucent, about 2 minutes. Add the wine and cook until reduced by half, 6 to 8 minutes, using a wooden spoon to scrape up the browned bits from the bottom of the pot.

4

Return the reserved herbs and meat to the pot. Add the tomatoes and their juices. Increase the heat to high and bring the liquid to a boil. Cover the pot and transfer it to the oven to cook for 2 hours, or until the meat is tender. Remove the pot from the oven, uncover, and let cool at room temperature for about an hour.

5

Remove the herbs and discard. Transfer the meat to a cutting board and chop finely, then return it to the sauce and stir to combine. Place 3 cups of sauce in the bottom of a very large serving bowl. Add the prepared spaghetti, and toss to coat. Add more sauce, if needed. To serve family-style, ladle more sauce over and top with grated Parmesan.

SERVES 12 TO 15

THIS RECIPE NEEDS NO EXPLANATION: OBVIOUSLY, GCM'S ORIGINAL THAI FOOD stall, Sticky Rice, serves sticky rice. When you eat at the counter, it comes out with every order, served in a little lidded bamboo basket about the size of a soup can. You open the basket to find a plastic bag containing a ball of rice grains that, true to its name, stick together as if glued. And in a sense, the rice grains are glued together by their abundant starch. The bond is strong enough that you can pull off a pinch of rice, dunk it in sauce or curry, and eat it with your fingers. It's rice as utensil.

sticky
RICE

SERVES 8

2 cups **glutinous** or **sweet rice**

Note: *Sticky rice is made from a special short-grain variety called glutinous or sweet rice—although it is gluten free and no sweeter than other rice. The rice must be soaked overnight, and it is steamed rather than boiled. If you don't have a steamer basket, you can improvise one by lining a metal colander with cheesecloth, setting the colander over a pot of boiling water, and covering it with a large lid.*

1

Rinse the rice with warm water until the water runs clear. Place it in a medium bowl, cover with an inch of water, and soak at room temperature overnight.

2

Drain the rice through a fine-mesh sieve. Bring a large pot of water to a boil over high heat. Line a steamer insert or bamboo basket with cheesecloth. Add the rice. Steam the rice over the boiling water for 15 minutes, then remove the lid and, using a spoon, turn over the rice. Replace the lid, and continue cooking for 10 to 15 minutes, until the rice is translucent and tender. Fluff with a fork and let rest for 5 minutes before serving.

THE GENEROUS BREAKFAST PLATES AT JOSE CHIQUITO COME LOADED WITH SIDES of pinto beans and rice—a standard option west of the Rockies or wherever *huevos rancheros* are served. Expectations aren't high—the beans and rice are filler, right? Except chef-owner Marlon Medina makes his versions of both better than they need to be. Take the rice. When that big plate of food slides across the counter, you think to yourself, "I'll skip the rice to save on carbs." But then you have a taste of the rice because the diced bell pepper Marlon simmers with it looks so good. And then you have another taste to try to figure out what else is in there. (Answer: pureed onions and garlic.) And by then you decide that rice, when it's this good, must be eaten.

Marlon spent nine years as a line cook at Jose Chiquito before he bought the business in 2016, saying at the time that he wanted to upgrade the food. He has. Red Pepper Rice goes to show that nothing is so simple it can't be improved.

2 cups **long-grain white rice**

½ medium **white onion**, diced

2 **garlic cloves**

1 teaspoon fine **sea salt**

2 tablespoons **vegetable oil**

1 medium **red bell pepper**, seeded and cut into ¼-inch dice

1
Rinse the rice with warm water until the water runs clear.

2
Combine the onion, garlic, salt, and 1 cup water in a blender or food processor. Blend until liquefied.

3
Heat the oil in a medium saucepan over high heat until a grain of rice dropped in crackles. Add the rest of the rice and toast, stirring, for 2 minutes. Add the liquefied aromatics, the bell pepper, and 2 cups water, and stir to combine.

4
Cover the pot, reduce the heat to low, and simmer for 20 minutes. Remove the pot from the heat, fluff the rice with a fork, and keep covered until ready to serve.

RED PEPPER

SERVES

8

★★★ RICE

seafood FRIED RICE

FRIED RICE GIVES NEW LIFE TO LEFTOVER COOKED RICE, WHICH OTHERWISE doesn't have much going for it. In fact, the recipe below from China Cafe won't turn out quite right if your rice is freshly cooked. On the other hand, it can be adapted to suit whatever other ingredients you have to work with. The recommended shrimp, scallops, and squid dress it up to be a halfway fancy dish, but they could be swapped out for leftovers from the fridge—like meat stripped from last night's roast chicken and whatever stray veggies are hanging around. Mix in a couple of scrambled eggs to bind the elements and give the dish added heft.

1 tablespoon **kosher salt**

Juice of ½ **lemon**

⅓ pound **bay scallops**

½ pound medium **shrimp**, peeled

½ pound **squid**, tubes cut into ¼-inch rounds, tentacles chopped

¼ cup **vegetable oil**

4 cups day-old **rice**

2 large **eggs**, beaten

1 teaspoon **chicken bouillon powder**, preferably Knorr

1 teaspoon **mushroom soy sauce**

1 teaspoon **oyster sauce**

½ teaspoon **sugar**

1½ cups **bean sprouts**

2 **scallions** (white and green parts), chopped

1 In a large saucepan, bring the salt, lemon juice, and 5 cups water to a boil over high heat. Add the scallops, shrimp, and squid. Reduce the heat to medium and simmer until the shrimp are pink and opaque, about 5 minutes. Drain everything.

2 Heat the oil in a wok or large skillet over high heat. When the oil shimmers, add the rice and eggs. Stir until the eggs are cooked, taking care to break them up and distribute the egg through the rice. Add the bouillon powder, soy sauce, oyster sauce, and sugar. Continue cooking until the sauces are absorbed. Add the cooked shellfish, bean sprouts, and scallions. Toss just until the ingredients are combined, and serve hot.

SERVES 4

ancient
GRAINS BOWL
WITH KOMBUCHA DRESSING

WITH ITS DARK GREENS, ANTIOXIDANT-RICH ORANGE VEGETABLES, ANCIENT grains, chard stems, and kombucha dressing, this recipe checks the boxes on a bunch of culinary trends. Superfoods! Quinoa! Zero waste! Fermenting! Bowls! But really, a bowl like this is just a strategy for pulling together several varied elements into a unified whole.

The wilted chard leaves and spinach become a warm salad that also includes sautéed chard stems, slivered carrots, and cubed butternut squash tossed with toasted spices. The light dressing takes advantage of kombucha's naturally sour vinegar taste and brings everything together. The base layer of cooked whole grains (such as teff or bulgur) plays off the topping of crunchy parched quinoa and provides a study in contrasting textures. As written, the recipe is vegan, but top it as you like: crumbled feta, a soft egg, or a piece of grilled salmon are natural moves. The bowl should be a total meal, compressed into one serving vessel.

¼ cup **quinoa**

2 tablespoons **extra-virgin olive oil**

2 **garlic cloves**, 1 lightly crushed and 1 minced

1 bunch **rainbow chard**, washed, leaves cut into 1½-inch ribbons (about 10 cups), and stems cut into 1-inch matchsticks

1 medium **carrot**, cut into 1½-inch matchsticks

1 teaspoon **kosher salt**, plus more as needed

10 tightly packed cups **spinach**, washed

1 medium **yellow onion**, chopped

2 cups (½-inch dice) peeled **butternut squash**

¼ teaspoon **cumin seeds**, toasted and ground

¼ teaspoon whole **coriander**, toasted and ground

1 teaspoon grated **fresh ginger**

Kombucha Dressing (recipe opposite)

2 cups **ancient grains** (teff, bulgur, spelt, kamut, etc.), prepared according to package instructions, kept warm

1

Place the quinoa in a small bowl and cover with water by 1 inch. Soak for 5 minutes. Drain it through a fine-mesh sieve. Rinse again and drain. Transfer quinoa to a small skillet, and toast over medium heat until deeply browned, 15 to 20 minutes—the quinoa will pop as it begins to toast. Transfer the quinoa to a small bowl, and set aside.

2

Heat 1 tablespoon olive oil in a large sauté pan over high heat. When it shimmers, add the crushed garlic and fry until golden, 1 minute. Add the chard stems, carrot, and ½ teaspoon of the salt, and sauté until the carrots are tender, 3 to 4 minutes. Transfer to a large serving bowl. Return the pan to the heat, and add half the chard leaves and ½ teaspoon of salt. Cover until the chard wilts, about 1 minute. Add the remaining chard and turn it to the bottom of the pan using kitchen tongs. Cover the pan for 1 minute more. When all the chard is wilted, leave it in the pan and repeat the wilting process with the spinach and more salt. After the final addition, remove the lid and continue cooking until the greens are silky, 2 to 3 minutes. Transfer to a colander placed over the sink to drain. Add the drained greens to the serving bowl with chard stems and carrots.

3

Wipe the pan from the greens clean and add 1 tablespoon olive oil over high heat. When the oil shimmers, add the onion and squash. Sauté until the squash is just tender, 8 to 10 minutes. Add the cumin, coriander, ginger, and minced garlic. Continue cooking until the garlic is fragrant, 1 minute more. Transfer to the serving bowl with the other vegetables.

4

To serve, sprinkle with half the toasted quinoa and pour the kombucha dressing on top. Toss to combine. Serve with the prepared ancient grains and the remaining quinoa alongside.

SERVES 8

KOMBUCHA DRESSING

MAKES ABOUT ½ CUP

¼ cup **extra-virgin olive oil**

¼ cup plain **kombucha**

½ teaspoon grated **lemon zest** or **tangerine zest**

1 teaspoon freshly squeezed **lemon juice**

¼ teaspoon **kosher salt**, plus more as needed

¼ teaspoon freshly ground **black pepper**, plus more as needed

In a small bowl, whisk together the olive oil, kombucha, lemon zest, lemon juice, salt, and pepper. Taste and adjust the seasoning, if needed. Store refrigerated in an airtight container for up to 3 days. The dressing will separate—whisk or shake before using.

GRILLED
MARGHERITA
PIZZA

AT OLIO WOOD-FIRED PIZZERIA, CHEF-OWNER BRAD KENT AND HIS CREW BAKE crisp-bottomed pizzas in an Italian wood-burning oven so heavy that structural engineers had to reinforce GCM's concrete flooring to support it. The oven reaches 800°F or more, and the pizzas achieve a perfectly char-spotted crust—Brad calls it "leoparding"—in less than three minutes. The result is almost impossible to duplicate at home, and few people have access to a wood-burning oven at all. But Brad's suggestion is to grill the pizza instead. A grill's intense heat stripes the crust and cooks the pizza in less than five minutes. What's more, stretching the dough for grilled pizza requires less finesse. You coat the dough and your hands with olive oil, and stretch it into shape on a lightly oiled baking sheet. (By the way, there is no law saying a grilled pizza has to be round.) Unlike oven-made pizza, this crust is grilled on one side *before* dressing it. When you flip it, you lay down a layer of cheese, *then* tomato sauce, so that the cheese melts from direct contact with the hot crust.

1 cup plus 2 tablespoons (260 grams) **filtered water**, at room temperature

3 cups plus 2 tablespoons (410 grams) unbleached **all-purpose flour** (Brad uses King Arthur brand), plus more for the work surface

2 teaspoons (6 grams) **sugar**

1 teaspoon (3 grams) **active dry yeast**

5 tablespoons (15 grams) **extra-virgin olive oil**, plus more for drizzling

2 teaspoons (6 grams) **sea salt**, plus more for finishing

½ cup grated **Grana Padano cheese**

6 ounces **mozzarella cheese**, torn

⅓ cup **tomato sauce**, store-bought or homemade (recipe follows)

8 to 10 fresh **basil** leaves

Notes: *This technique for pizza dough looks more complicated than it is because Brad gives specific instructions for every move you'll make. Don't be daunted. The recipe requires a two-day process, but less than an hour of that is active time in the kitchen. The remainder is to let the dough rise and develop flavor. Yes, mastering pizza requires some practice, but this dough comes as close as possible to being fail-safe.*

If you already have practice making pizzas in the oven, this dough will also work beautifully for oven-baked pies.

1

In the bowl of a stand mixer fitted with a dough hook attachment, combine the water, flour, sugar, and yeast. Mix for 2 minutes on the lowest speed. Drizzle 1 tablespoon of the oil over the dough, and sprinkle the salt evenly over the top. Cover the bowl with aluminum foil, and let the dough rest in a warm place for 20 minutes.

2

Remove the foil, and mix the dough for 7 minutes on the lowest speed until it is glossy. Cover the bowl with foil again, and let rest at room temperature for 1½ hours. Using your hands, shape the dough into a ball. Return it to the bowl, cover the bowl with foil, and place in the refrigerator for 24 hours.

3

Remove the dough from the refrigerator. Punch it down, and reshape it into a ball. Cover the bowl with foil again, and return it to the refrigerator to rest for at least another 12 hours, or until ready to use.

4

From 2 to 4 hours before serving, remove the dough from the refrigerator, and transfer it to a lightly floured work surface. Divide the dough into 2 equal portions, and shape each half into a ball. Arrange the balls 4 inches apart on a baking sheet, and cover tightly with plastic wrap. Set aside at room temperature to rise until doubled in bulk, 2 to 4 hours.

RECIPE CONTINUES

5

Heat the grill to medium.

6

Stretch the dough. Leave one ball of the dough on the baking sheet, coat the other with 1 tablespoon of oil, and coat your hands as well. Gently stretch and pull the dough to form a 12-inch round. Lay the stretched dough directly on the grill's rack. Cook for 2 minutes, or until the bottom is lightly browned. Flip the dough. Sprinkle with half the cheeses, then top with half the tomato sauce. Cover the grill, and cook until the cheese melts, 2 to 4 minutes. Transfer the pizza to a serving platter. Drizzle 1 tablespoon olive oil over the top. Finish with a sprinkle of sea salt and half the fresh basil leaves. Repeat the process to make the second pizza.

MAKES 2 13-INCH PIZZAS

OLIO'S TOMATO SAUCE

2½ cups canned **crushed tomatoes**

2½ cups canned **whole peeled tomatoes**

2 tablespoons **extra-virgin olive oil**

½ teaspoon freshly ground **black pepper**

1 teaspoon **sea salt**

Scant ½ teaspoon dried **oregano**

2 cups tightly packed fresh **basil** leaves

1

Place the crushed and whole tomatoes in a food processor or blender. Pulse briefly to puree, being careful not to overprocess and break up the seeds. Working in 1-cup batches, strain the puree through a fine-mesh sieve placed over a medium bowl. Press the puree through to remove the seeds, discarding them.

2

Whisk the oil, pepper, salt, and oregano into the tomatoes. Stir in the basil leaves. Cover the bowl, and place in the refrigerator overnight to allow the flavors to meld.

3

Strain the sauce through a colander placed over a large bowl. Discard the basil leaves. Store refrigerated in an airtight container for up to 3 days.

MAKES 4½ CUPS

OLIO CHEF-OWNER Brad Kent
is nothing if not precise, as his highly detailed
instructions for pizza dough prove. In the Olio
kitchen at GCM, Brad weighs out his ingredients to
the gram and times each step of the process to the
second. Brad also has specific opinions about the
best brand of flour, olive oil, canned tomatoes, and
even the water for a perfect pizza. It almost goes
without saying that your homemade version of Olio's
pizza dough will turn out a *little* bit different than the
results Brad gets when he makes it himself. But that's
okay. Perfection is an ideal and it takes practice to
get there. For home cooks who want to come as close
as possible to duplicating Brad's scientific recipe—
and who have a digital scale and his penchant for
accuracy—metric weight measurements are given in
the ingredients list alongside the standard volume
measures on page 137.

One more note: Stretching the dough is often
the trickiest part of making pizza. Brad's advice on
the process applies universally, whatever recipe
you're using. "Don't activate the gluten," he says. "It's
like a sleeping baby." What he means is that gluten,
a wheat protein that provides elasticity, is quiet
and malleable as long as you handle it gently—very
gently. If you try to stretch the dough too vigorously,
too fast, or too far by yanking it in various directions,
the gluten will "wake up" and become difficult to
work. "Like a baby when you wake it up, you can't
quiet it down," Brad explains. At that point you'll
never get the dough stretched properly, unless you
lay it aside for 30 minutes, long enough for the gluten
to relax and "go back to sleep."

HAPPY HOUR

HAPPY HOUR AT THE MARKET BEGINS WHENEVER PEOPLE WANT IT TO: IT'S NOT unusual to see groups of friends drinking wine in the mid-afternoon, especially on weekends, and a morning beer makes perfect sense to someone who comes in at the end of a night shift. But typically, of course, it's the end of the work day when the Market fills up with people ready to recuperate from their hours in the office. By then, lunch has long passed, and they're craving a little snack—something that's satisfyingly salty-spicy-crunchy, like these pepitas, or pumpkin seeds, toasted with cayenne pepper and spices. The recipe was inspired by the bins of dry goods at Valeria's, a destination for Latino specialty products, including a dozen or more types of dried chiles. A handful of pepitas with a cocktail will take the edge off your hunger, while you contemplate the most important decision of the day—what's for dinner?

SPICY PEPITAS

1 tablespoon **peanut oil**

1 **garlic clove**, crushed

2 tablespoons grated **piloncillo** or **turbinado sugar**

1½ teaspoons **kosher salt**

½ teaspoon ground **cayenne pepper**

½ teaspoon toasted ground **cumin seeds**

¼ teaspoon freshly ground **black pepper**

1½ cups hulled **green pumpkin seeds** (8 ounces)

Note: *Piloncillo is unrefined cane sugar pressed into solid, cone-shaped blocks. You grate off the amount you need using a box grater. Turbinado, muscovado, or Demerara sugar could be substituted. The pepitas can be swapped out for peanuts or pecans.*

1

Combine the peanut oil and crushed garlic in a medium bowl, and set aside for 15 minutes. Combine the sugar, salt, and spices in a small bowl.

2

Add the pumpkin seeds to the garlic and oil, and toss to coat. Add the spice mixture, and toss to combine. Set aside for 30 minutes, stirring occasionally, to allow the flavors to meld.

3

Preheat the oven to 325°F. Spread out the seeds in a single layer on a parchment-lined baking sheet. Transfer to the oven and bake until toasted, 15 to 20 minutes. Remove from the oven and let cool—the pepitas will crackle as they do so. Serve warm or at room temperature. Store in an airtight container for up to a week.

MAKES 1½ CUPS

VALERIA'S, located at the center of the Market, is a chile mecca. The smells emanating from the open bins—warm, smoky, fruity—stop you in your tracks. There are cayenne peppers and chiles de árbol, smoked chipotles and *moritas*, shiny New Mexico chiles, wrinkly poblanos, and pea-size tepín chiles. This last variety, costing $60 per pound, is harvested from the wild. Birds, which aren't affected by capsaicin's heat, spread the seeds, hence the common English name, "bird chiles."

Valeria's also sells Latin pantry staples, such as dried beans, masa, posole, *piloncillo* (pressed brown sugar), and dried spices, as well as more exotic items like whole dried shrimp, wild-harvest pine nuts from New Mexico, and toasted grasshoppers (the delicacy *chapulines*).

From a larger historical perspective, the selection at Valeria's is a living museum of New World ingredients, foods that defined the cuisines of the Americas in the centuries before Christopher Columbus. In particular, corn, beans, and squash (including pumpkins) were a holy trinity to many cultures throughout North and South American. All three crops were soon taken back to Europe—along with New World chiles, chocolate, tomatoes, and potatoes—and quickly spread to more distant continents. Cuisines were transformed around the world; today we think of red chiles as intrinsic to Korean kimchi and tomatoes as fundamental to Italian pizza. Both were unknown in those countries before the opening of the so-called Columbian Exchange in 1492. In return, the New World got oranges, lemons, limes, apples, garlic, and spices from around the globe.

herb~TAHINI DIP

MADCAPRA PRACTICES THE VEGETABLE VERSION OF SNOUT-TO-TAIL COOKING BY working with all parts of the plant, including the "ugly bits" that other people would throw away, like beet stems and cauliflower cores. Co-owner Sarah Hymanson once fermented a delicious relish of shriveled late-summer beans. This recipe was developed to use herb stems, which are just as aromatic as the leaves. If you follow it as written, the result is a dip for crudités. Thin it out with a bit more water to get a drizzling sauce for grilled vegetables or meats, or use it as a dressing for greens. Basically, it goes well with everything.

MAKES

3

CUPS

12 fresh **parsley** sprigs, leaves and stems

7 fresh **mint** sprigs, leaves and stems

3 fresh **basil** sprigs, leaves and stems

5 fresh **cilantro** sprigs, leaves and stems

1 **garlic clove**, grated on a Microplane

2 teaspoons **kosher salt**

1¼ cups **tahini paste**

⅓ cup freshly squeezed **lemon juice** or **white wine vinegar**

Crudités, **pita chips**, and **oil-cured olives**, for serving

Combine the herbs, garlic, and salt in a blender or food processor. Pulse briefly until coarsely pureed. Add the tahini and lemon juice. Pulse until smooth, taking care not to overheat the mixture. With the motor running, slowly stream in 1¼ cups water to emulsify. Add more water until your desired consistency is reached. Serve with thinly sliced crudités, pita chips, and a dish of oil-cured olives.

GIARDINIERE

WHEN YOU THINK OF A PICKLE, WHAT COMES TO MIND? PROBABLY SOME VERSION of a pickled cucumber—the relish on a hot dog, a sandwich pickle, a kosher dill spear. It's a condiment, right? Bruce Kalman of Knead & Co thinks differently about pickles. He'll marinate a garden's worth of mixed vegetables and put them at the center of the plate. This recipe for his signature giardiniere is an appetizer in itself, especially when served with crusty bread and a slab of cultured butter.

2 cups **white wine vinegar**

2 tablespoons **organic sugar**

2 tablespoons fine **sea salt**

3 **serrano chiles**, stems removed

¾ cup (1-inch-dice) **red bell peppers**

½ cup julienned **yellow onions**

1¾ cups **cauliflower** florets

1¼ cups thinly sliced **carrots**

1 cup thinly sliced **celery**, with leaves

2 tablespoons finely chopped **garlic**

2 teaspoons **yellow mustard seeds**

2 teaspoons dried **oregano**

¼ cup **extra-virgin olive oil**

1

Combine the vinegar, sugar, and salt in a large stainless steel saucepan over medium heat. When the sugar and salt have dissolved, add the chiles, and cook over medium heat until they turn dull green, 6 to 8 minutes. Remove the pan from the heat, and allow the ingredients to cool to room temperature. Remove the chiles from the brine, reserving it, and slice them into ½-inch rounds.

2

Combine the sliced chiles, bell peppers, onions, cauliflower, carrot, celery, garlic, mustard seed, oregano, and olive oil in a large bowl. Stir to mix. Pour the reserved brine over the vegetables. Cover and allow to marinate in the refrigerator for 3 days before using. Store refrigerated in an airtight container for up to 2 weeks.

MAKES ABOUT 2 PINTS

DELI DILLS

THIS RECIPE IS CHEF MICAH WEXLER'S TAKE ON THE CLASSIC KOSHER DILL pickle. He ferments the cucumbers whole over the course of a week or more, during which time they develop the tangy, yeasty flavor typical of lacto-fermented pickles. A fistful of fresh dill and whole heads of garlic season the brine. The grape leaves, while optional, help the pickles stay crisp. Micah cuts the cured pickles into spears to serve alongside sandwiches, but they could also be sliced into rounds, chopped into dill relish, or, of course, eaten whole out of the jar.

4¼ pounds **pickling cucumbers**

1 bunch fresh **dill**

1 to 1½ whole heads of **garlic**, cut in half crosswise

4 jarred **grape leaves**, drained (optional)

¼ cup plus 1 tablespoon **pickling spice**

5½ quarts **bottled water**

1⅓ cups **Diamond Crystal kosher salt**

Notes: *The fermentation process can take up to 2 weeks for the pickles to sour. Use bottled water because the chlorine in tap water can interrupt the beneficial microbes that cause fermentation. The weight of salt by volume varies considerably depending on its texture: A cup of flaky kosher salt weighs less than a cup of fine sea salt, and even different brands of kosher salt vary. Use Diamond Crystal salt, as specified, to ensure proper measurement and consistent results.*

It's not unusual to find a tiny speck of white, gray, or black mold forming inside a container of pickles as they ferment. Don't worry. Just spoon it out and discard. No harm done.

1 Wash the cucumbers thoroughly. Cut a ⅛-inch round off the blossom end, opposite the stem end; if in doubt, trim both ends. Place the cucumbers in a large nonreactive container, such as a crock or a food-grade plastic bucket. Layer in the dill, garlic, grape leaves, if using, and pickling spice.

2 In a separate large container, stir the salt into half the bottled water until it dissolves. Add the remaining water.

3 Pour the salt-water brine over the cucumbers. Leave at room temperature, uncovered, for 2 to 3 days. Cover with a lid and transfer to the refrigerator to cure for 1 to 2 weeks. Once cured, store for up to 2 weeks.

MAKES 1 GALLON

SANDOR KATZ, a self-proclaimed "fermentation revivalist," helped make fermenting trendy with his bestselling books. When he came to GCM's 2016 Pickle Party, a kraut mob of hundreds showed up for his workshop to make 1,000 pounds of the stuff in a single busy morning. That same day, Micah Wexler was selling his fermented kosher dill pickles from a bucket on the counter at Wexler's Deli. Micah would be first to admit that the art of fermentation is trendy, but it's nothing new. In fact, the kosher dills at Wexler's Deli are much the same as those made one hundred years ago in the Jewish immigrant neighborhoods of New York's Lower East Side. This recipe isn't just an example of "fermentation revivalism," but also an act of cultural continuity.

NEXT TO THE CHEESE COUNTER AT DTLA CHEESE IS A SMALL KITCHEN, WHERE chef Reed Herrick makes his "cheese-based cuisine." The bestseller is Cheesy Potatoes, a creative riff on a Swiss après-ski snack. In the traditional version, a large hunk of alpine cow's-milk cheese called *raclette* is warmed next to an open fire. As the edge melts, it's scraped onto a little plate and passed around with potatoes and tart pickles as a sociable snack with drinks before dinner. Reed's more kitchen-friendly approach tops roasted peewee potatoes with grated Spanish sheep's-milk cheese, then spicy romesco sauce. It can also be turned into a full meal by adding a layer of fried chorizo or crispy shrimp (or both) beneath the cheese before the pan goes into the oven.

2 pounds mixed **heirloom peewee potatoes**

2 tablespoons **extra-virgin olive oil**

3 **garlic cloves**, crushed

¼ teaspoon fine **sea salt**

½ teaspoon **Espelette pepper** or **sweet paprika**

8 ounces **Idiazábal** or **Manchego cheese**, grated (2 cups)

Romesco sauce, store-bought or homemade (recipe follows)

Note: *Espelette pepper is a mild, lightly smoky, subtly sweet chile powder made from piment d'Espelette peppers. Sweet paprika would be an acceptable substitute, but Spanish pimentón and other smoked paprika are too smoky.*

1

Preheat the oven to 400°F.

2

Scrub the potatoes and dry them well. In a large bowl, toss the potatoes with the olive oil, garlic, salt, and Espelette pepper. Spread them on a parchment-lined baking sheet, transfer them to the oven, and roast, turning occasionally, for 30 to 45 minutes, or until tender when pierced with a fork (total cooking time will depend on the size of the potatoes). Remove the potatoes from the oven, and increase the temperature to 500°F.

3

Transfer the potatoes to a large cast-iron skillet or ovenproof baking dish. Cover with the grated cheese, return to the oven, and bake until the cheese melts and starts to brown, about 10 minutes. If the top doesn't brown enough, run the dish under the broiler for a minute or two. Drizzle with romesco sauce, and serve extra sauce on the side.

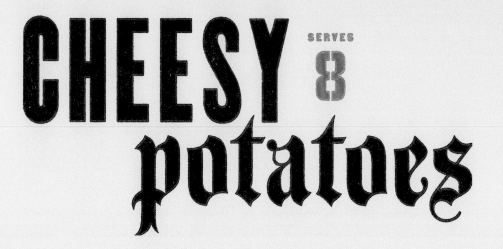

CHEESY potatoes

SERVES 8

RECIPE CONTINUES

ROMESCO
SAUCE

MAKES ABOUT 2 CUPS

½ cup **extra-virgin olive oil**

2 tablespoons finely sliced **garlic**

3 **red bell peppers**, roasted, peeled, and seeded (see page 85)

¼ cup **Marcona almonds**, toasted

½ teaspoon **Espelette pepper** (see note on previous page)

¼ cup **sherry vinegar**

Kosher salt

1

Combine the oil and sliced garlic in a small sauté pan over low heat, and toast until the garlic is golden, 1 to 2 minutes. Remove the pan from the heat.

2

Combine the roasted bell peppers, almonds, Espelette, vinegar, and 2 pinches of salt in a blender or food processor. Pulse until smooth. With the motor running, stream in the garlic oil. Taste and adjust the seasonings, if needed. Store refrigerated in an airtight container for up to a week.

SISTERS LYDIA AND MARNIE CLARKE,

the cofounders of DTLA Cheese, call themselves "curd nerds" and are well known in the close-knit world of professional cheesemongers as "SoCal dairy aristocracy." That's because in 1945 their grandfather Harold Stueve and his brothers established Alta Dena Dairy, which championed drive-through dairy bars and other innovations. Stueve was more than just a successful businessman, however. He also became a passionate advocate for natural foods, expanding Alta Dena's offerings with fermented dairy products such as kefir and spearheading the progressive concept of "healthy milk" from healthy cows. He also took a fierce public stand to defend consumers' right to buy unpasteurized "raw" milk. A decades-long legal and political battle ensued. Stueve won the battle (California law still permits the sale of raw milk), but it cost him the company. Personal bankruptcy forced the family to sell Alta Dena Dairy in the 1990s to a giant dairy conglomerate.

Today Harold Stueve's progressive spirit lives on with Lydia and Marnie. In 2010, they opened their first business, the Cheese Cave, in Claremont, east of Los Angeles, where they sold over two hundred varieties of American farmhouse cheeses, classic European artisanal cheeses—and raw milk. When the sisters and Lydia's boyfriend, Reed Herrick, brought their dairy game to GCM in 2013, DTLA Cheese became the first full-scale cheese shop to open Downtown in a generation. One or both sisters can usually be found behind the counter. (Both are petite and stand on footstools to peer over the top of their cheese-packed display cases.)

CHEESE
PLATTER

THE IDEA OF "SEASONALITY" IS USUALLY APPLIED TO FRUITS
and vegetables, because the produce available at a farmer's market
(or a farm-to-table restaurant) obviously varies with the seasons. But
Lydia Clarke, who started DTLA Cheese with her sister, Marnie, and
her boyfriend, Reed Herrick, explains that cheeses have their seasons,
too. Late spring and early summer see the arrival of fresh soft, mild
cheeses. Summer brings bloomy rind cheeses. Firmer alpine cheeses
mature in late fall. And the most fully aged cheeses, including
cloth-wrapped Cheddars and cave-aged blues, go with cold weather.
The cheese platters Lydia assembles at DTLA likewise vary with the
seasons. There's usually a sweet element, such as quince paste or
honeycomb. Often she'll add a few salted Marcona almonds. Crisp
crackers are never wrong. But Lydia's signature might be the
paper-thin slices of dehydrated apples, pears, and oranges she tucks
alongside the cheese, whatever the season.

ARTICHOKE HOT "wings"

THE KITCHEN AT GOLDEN ROAD MAKES ITS OWN MARINATED ARTICHOKE HEARTS in-house, and they leave the stems long. Once the hearts are quartered, battered, fried, and doused with hot sauce, they really do look like chicken wings. Store-bought marinated quartered artichoke hearts will wind up looking more like artichoke poppers. But in any case, this recipe proves that vegan cuisine is more than just hippie health food—it's delicious, mainstream, and on-trend.

1½ cups **all-purpose flour**

1½ teaspoons **garlic powder**

½ teaspoon **chili powder**

1 cup **lager beer**

3 cups **panko bread crumbs**

Oil, for frying

2 12-ounce jars marinated quartered **artichoke hearts**

Store-bought **buffalo wing sauce**

3 cups **vegan mayonnaise**, such as Vegenaise

3 tablespoons dried **parsley**

1 tablespoon dried **dill**

1 teaspoon **onion powder**

2 tablespoon **apple cider vinegar**

2 to 3 tablespoons freshly squeezed **lemon juice**

Fresh **celery** sticks, **carrot** sticks, and/or **Giardiniere** (page 146), for serving

1

In a large bowl, whisk together the flour, ½ teaspoon of the garlic powder, and the chili powder. Whisk in the beer to make a smooth, thin batter. Place the panko in a medium bowl.

2

Pour 2 inches of oil into a large saucepan or enameled casserole and heat to 375°F over high heat. Drain the artichoke hearts, and pat them dry. Dredge each quarter in the batter, allowing any excess to drip off, then roll them through the panko, pressing it to adhere.

3

Working in batches, carefully lower several of the battered artichokes into the hot oil. Fry until golden brown, turning over once or twice, about 3 minutes total. Transfer to a paper-towel-lined tray to drain. Transfer the wings to a large bowl, sprinkle generously with wing sauce, and toss well.

4

In a small bowl, whisk together the vegan mayo, parsley, dill, the remaining 1 teaspoon garlic powder, the onion powder, vinegar, and lemon juice. Serve the "wings" with the vegan ranch dressing, fresh veggies, and/or pickled vegetables alongside.

SERVES 6 TO 8 AS AN APPETIZER

OYSTERS
ON A CLOUD

THE OYSTER GOURMET

STALL
E-13

THE FRENCHMAN BEHIND GCM'S OYSTER GOURMET OYSTER BAR, CHRISTOPHE
Happillon, describes himself as the only *maître ecailler* (certified shellfish master) in Los
Angeles. He says the best way to appreciate the range of flavors produced by oysters from
different waters is to taste them side by side—a creamy Grassy Bar from central California
versus a crisp Hama Hama from Washington State versus a briny Sol Azul from Baja. Once
you find a favorite oyster variety, use this recipe to intensify its profile by garnishing the half
shell with a bit of oyster foam. Christophe calls the recipe *huitres à l'écume,* which could be
translated literally as "oysters in foam" or even "foamed oysters." But the true Frenchman
has a touch of the romantic about him, so the fanciful name Oysters on a Cloud is perhaps
most fitting.

12 medium **oysters** (each about
4½ inches long)

1 **egg white**

Pinch of **white pepper**

1 ounce **caviar** or **salmon roe**

1
Place a small bowl and a whisk in
the freezer to chill.

2
Shuck the oysters over a large
bowl to catch all the liquids. Add
the shucked oysters to the bowl.
Reserve the bottom shell of each
oyster—the deeper, cupped one.
Keep the oysters in the fridge
until you're ready for them.

3
Measure out ¼ cup of the oyster
liquor, and strain it through a
fine-mesh sieve into the chilled
mixing bowl. Add the egg
white and white pepper. Whisk
vigorously to soft peaks. Chill the
foam in the fridge for 30 minutes;
it will firm up.

4
To serve, place the oyster meat
back into the reserved half shells.
Top each with a teaspoon of the
foam and ½ teaspoon of caviar or
salmon roe.

**MAKES A DOZEN
OYSTERS**

Happy Hour **157**

OYSTER SHOOTERS

THIS DISH MAKES AN EYE-CATCHING PRESENTATION AND IS LESS COMPLICATED than it might appear. Basically, the idea is to soak the oysters in a booze-infused marinade, then layer them in a glass with colorful garnishes and douse them with an Asian-inflected mignonette sauce. Think of it as garnished oysters on the half shell, but served as a shooter—which just means you can prep them ahead of time, before guests arrive.

You can find most of the ingredients for this recipe under one roof at a typical Asian market. *Tobiko* is beautiful orange Japanese flying fish roe. Yuzu, a fragrant citrus, gets absorbed by the daikon so it isn't as . . . radishy. Sesame chili oil has a spicy roasted sesame quality. Baby mizuna is subtly grassy-peppery. Flavor on flavor on flavor.

½ cup **vodka**

1 cup **mirin**

Zest of 1 **lemon**

1 teaspoon grated fresh **ginger**

⅓ cup **fish sauce**

16 live **oysters** in the shell

1½ cups **rice vinegar**

½ head of **fennel**, thinly shaved and diced, fronds reserved

¼ teaspoon freshly ground **black pepper**, tied in a cheesecloth

2½ cups **ice water**

1 teaspoon bottled **yuzu juice**

Pinch of fine **sea salt**

7 ounces **daikon**

4 ounces **tobiko**

Sesame chili oil

Hawaiian black salt and **baby mizuna greens**, for garnish

Note: *This recipe requires an overnight infusion for the vodka base, and the oysters marinate for 2 hours before serving.*

1

In a small bowl, whisk together the vodka, ⅓ cup of the mirin, the lemon zest, and the ginger. Cover and refrigerate overnight. The next day, strain the infused vodka through a fine-mesh sieve, discarding the solids.

2

Marinate the oysters: Whisk the infused vodka with ⅓ cup of the mirin and the fish sauce in a medium bowl. Shuck the oysters over a large bowl to catch their liquids. Add the oysters and their liquor to the marinade and refrigerate, covered, for 2 hours.

3

Meanwhile, make the mignonette: Combine the rice vinegar and the remaining ⅓ cup mirin in a bowl, then add the diced fennel and black pepper. Cover and set aside for 2 hours.

4

Make the daikon garnish: Combine the ice water and yuzu juice with a pinch of salt in a medium bowl. Using the julienne attachment on your mandoline or a spiralizer, cut the daikon into ribbons. Plunge the ribbons into the water bath. Chill for 20 minutes in the refrigerator to curl the daikon ribbons.

5

To assemble, place 1 teaspoon of tobiko in the bottom of a shooter glass. Using a slotted spoon, gently lay 1 oyster in each glass. Add ⅛ teaspoon of the fennel from the mignonette with a bit of the liquid. Top with 2 or 3 drops of chili oil. Garnish each glass with a tangle of daikon, a few strands of chopped fennel frond, several grains of black salt, and a pinch of baby mizuna.

MAKES 16 SHOOTERS

COCKTAIL
"FAMILIES"

THE CONVENTIONAL BARTENDER WAS A DRINKS SLINGER. BUT NOW, PROBABLY for the first time in the modern era, top mixologists carry clout in the food world, and chefs have embraced cocktails as an element of the overall culinary experience. Today's mixologists think about their creations in terms of seasonality, farm-to-table sustainability, and other culinary priorities. The duo behind Courage & Craft, Nicholas Krok and Ryan Duffy, were trained in the world of high-end craft cocktails before they opened their specialty liquor store at GCM. In designing the recipes below, Courage & Craft wanted to focus on cocktail "families," which sketch out basic recipes that someone can easily adapt to taste. Don't like gin in your Maid? Replace it with vodka or tequila or whatever else you like. These three families also use seasonal fruit and vegetables as a tribute to SoCal's farmer's markets.

NO. 1
THE FIX

The Fix family is a subset of the Sour family, a large category of citrus-flavored drinks that includes the margarita. What distinguishes the Fix is that it's served over crushed ice.

¾ ounce freshly squeezed **lemon juice**

¼ ounce **simple syrup** (see Note)

2 ounces **bourbon** or other spirit

2 to 4 tablespoons sliced seasonal **fruit**

 1
Combine all the ingredients in a shaker. Muddle the fruit. Dry-shake the ingredients (i.e., without ice) to blend.

2
Strain into a double old-fashioned glass filled with crushed ice.

MAKES 1

NO. 2
THE BUCK

The Buck is a category of cocktails made with carbonated soda. A famous one is the Moscow mule.

1 ounce freshly squeezed **lime juice**

¾ ounce **ginger syrup** (see Note)

2 ounces **tequila**, **mescal**, or other spirit

2 ounces **soda water**

Slice of **lime** and a piece of crystallized **ginger**, for garnish

1
Combine all the ingredients except the garnishes in a shaker with ice. Shake at a medium strength for about 5 seconds. Remove the cap, and pour the soda in with the other ingredients.

2
Strain into a collins glass filled with ice. Garnish with a lime wheel and candied ginger.

MAKES 1

Note: *To make simple syrup, combine 1 cup water and 1 cup sugar in a small saucepan over low heat. Stir until the sugar has dissolved. Store any unused syrup in the refrigerator. Also, if you can't find store-bought ginger syrup for the Buck, replace ginger syrup with ¼ ounce simple syrup and replace the soda water with 2½ ounces ginger beer.*

NO. 3
THE MAID

The starting point for the Maid family—mint leaves and cucumber muddled in the glass—also leads you to mojitos.

1 ounce freshly squeezed **lime juice**

¾ ounce **simple syrup** (see Note)

3 ¼-inch **cucumber** slices

6 to 8 fresh **mint** leaves

2 ounces **gin** or other spirit

Fresh **mint** sprig and **cucumber** slice, for garnish

1
Combine the lime juice, simple syrup, cucumber slices, and mint in a shaker. Lightly muddle the cucumber and mint, trying not to tear or break the mint, just press. Add the gin and ice. Shake at a medium strength for about 5 seconds.

2
Use a cocktail (or tea) strainer to double strain the mixture into a double old-fashioned glass filled with ice. Garnish with a mint sprig poked through a cucumber slice to look like a flower.

MAKES 1

HOWEVER YOU EXPLAIN THE RECENT TREND FOR COLD-PRESSED JUICE—AND IN some LA neighborhoods, cold-pressed juice bars are nearly as common as third-wave coffee bars—juicing definitely benefits from its perception as a "healthy choice," one that fits in naturally with vegetarian and vegan diets. But as GCM's co-creative director Joseph Shuldiner, author of the cookbook *Pure Vegan,* says, "Vodka is vegan." Press Brothers Juicery's watermelon slushy makes the same point. Spike the slushy with booze for a cocktail that turns happy hour into happy *and* healthy hour.

WATERMELON slushy

SERVES 2

2½ pounds (1-inch chunks) peeled **watermelon** (about 7 cups), preferably Sugar Baby or Icebox

1 small **lime**, quartered

½ ounce fresh **mint** leaves

14 ounces **ice**

3 ounces **gin** or **vodka** (optional)

Fresh **mint** sprig, for garnish

Note: *Making a slushy requires a juicer and a blender. But to make a non-slushy watermelon cocktail, just shake the juice and liquor in a cocktail shaker with a handful of ice, and strain into a glass. You can also freeze the watermelon base—it makes excellent ice pops.*

1

Consult the manufacturer's instructions for the operation of your particular juicer. The general technique is to feed pieces into the juicer one at a time, alternating juicy bits (watermelon) with more fibrous ones (lime, mint); the watermelon will flush out the fibrous pulp to keep the juicer from clogging. Fiber and froth will collect in the strainer, so use a wooden spoon to push aside the solids, allowing the juice to flow more readily. Empty the strainer when the pulp completely blocks the flow.

2

Put the ice in a blender, and pour in the juice and liquor, if using. Pulse for 30 seconds, or until the consistency is slushy. Serve immediately, garnished with a mint sprig.

VENDORS AT GCM CAN'T SERVE COCKTAILS BECAUSE OF CITY REGULATIONS. BUT if they could, someone surely would offer a Paloma, perhaps the best cocktail to accompany tacos. (Sorry, margarita.) This version is made with smoky mescal instead of the standard tequila, and is served in a glass rimmed with smoked salt.

Lime wedges

Smoked salt

3 ounces freshly squeezed grapefruit **juice**

⅓ ounce freshly squeezed **lime juice**

2 ounces **mescal** or **tequila**

Dash of **orange bitters**

2 ounces **seltzer water**

1

Rub the rim of a tall glass with a lime wedge, then dip the rim into a small dish of smoked salt. Fill the glass with ice.

2

Combine the grapefruit juice, lime juice, mescal, and bitters in a cocktail pitcher. Pour the mixture over the ice in the glass. Top with the seltzer water. Garnish with a fresh lime wedge.

MAKES 1

SMOKY PALOMA

michelada

NOWHERE IN GRAND CENTRAL MARKET IS THE THEATER OF THE KITCHEN MORE dramatic than at Villa Moreliana, a taco stall at the Broadway entrance. The house specialty is *carnitas,* chunks of pork simmered in lard for hours. Villa Moreliana makes it daily in quantities that boggle the mind. The standard cooking pot is a copper *cazo* larger than an antique washtub. Villa Moreliana does everything the traditional way, meaning all cuts of the hog cook together—the shoulder, the skin, the tongue. The customer then asks for either a particular cut or *surtida,* "mixed," and the *taquero* chops the meat in front of your eyes. You pay at the cashier, sluice some salsa on your tacos, and find a seat at the counter to watch the spectacle of simmering cauldrons of pork. What you want to drink at that moment is a Michelada, the Mexican cocktail of beer cut with seasoned tomato juice. It's the best way to relieve a hangover—or to start working on one.

Lime wedges

Kosher salt

Pinch of **ground cayenne pepper**

1 12-ounce bottle Pacifico or Corona **beer**, ice cold

8 ounces **Bloody Mary base**, store-bought or homemade (see page 71)

1

Rub the rims of 2 pint glasses with a lime wedge, and dip the rims in a small dish of salt mixed with a pinch of cayenne. Fill the glasses with ice.

2

Combine the beer and Bloody Mary base in a cocktail pitcher, and pour the mixture into the glasses. Garnish with a lime wedge.

SERVES 2

AGUA DE TUNA
(PRICKLY PEAR LIMEADE)

TORRES PRODUCE, ONE OF TWO GREENGROCERS AT GRAND CENTRAL MARKET, carries prickly pear in two forms: the paddles (nopales) and the fruit (*tunas*). Tunas come in several colors, all seedy. A good use for the red ones is this lightweight but deeply colored *agua fresca,* which literally means "fresh water." *Fresca* also carries the additional connotations of pure, sweet, cool, and clear—a perfect description of the drink itself.

1 pound (about 6) **prickly pear** fruits (tunas) or other seasonal fruit

Juice from 2 **limes** or **lemons**

1 cup **sugar**, or to taste

Notes: *Store-bought tunas are de-spined, but you'll want to wear gloves to peel them just in case any of the tiny hairlike spines remain.*

This recipe can also be made with other fruits, including pineapple, guava, watermelon, and strawberry. Adjust the sugar to taste, depending on the fruit.

1
Peel and quarter the fruits. Puree them in a blender or food processor until liquefied, then strain it through a fine-mesh sieve, discarding the seeds.

2
Combine the fruit juice, citrus juice, and 2 quarts water in a pitcher. Stir in the sugar to taste. Serve chilled.

SERVES 8

MADCAPRA CHEFS SARA KRAMER AND SARAH HYMANSON TOOK AN EXTENSIVE research trip through Israel in the months before they opened their falafel stand at GCM. One of the best inspirations they brought back was for a homemade soda that played the earthy flavor of beets against the citrusy taste of sumac. From a distance, the soda is nearly indistinguishable from another popular hot-weather drink sold by GCM taco vendors—*agua de jamaica* (hibiscus tea). The taste of beets is unmistakable, however, even when lightened with soda water. A splash of vodka transforms the soda into a hot-weather cocktail.

1¼ cups **sugar**

½ cup ground **sumac**

½ cup **beet juice** (see Note)

1⅓ cups freshly squeezed **lemon juice** (4 to 6 lemons)

6 ounces **vodka** (optional)

40 ounces **soda water**

SPIKED BEET-SUMAC SODA SERVES 8

Note: *To make beet juice in a blender or food processor, peel and chop three raw beets into ½-inch pieces. Add ½ cup water, and pulse until liquefied. Strain the puree through a damp jelly bag or two layers of wet cheesecloth that has been wetted and wrung out.*

1

Combine 2¾ cups water, the sugar, and the sumac in a small saucepan, and bring to a boil over medium heat. Reduce the heat to low, cover, and simmer for 20 minutes. Strain into a medium bowl through a damp jelly bag or a double layer of cheesecloth that has been wetted and wrung out.

2

Combine the sumac syrup, beet juice, lemon juice, and vodka, if using, in a pitcher. Fill 8 tall glasses with ice. Pour the sumac-beet mixture into the glasses, and top with soda water.

MEAT & FISH

THIS WARM ALBACORE SALAD, A MARKET CLASSIC THAT'S EASY TO REPLICATE at home, plays on Prawn's signature theme of sustainable seafood prepared in high-temperature steam kettles. You quickly cook the fish in broth seasoned with sautéed onions, shiitake mushrooms, dates, and preserved lemon peel. Then you pour it over shredded napa cabbage and mustard; the broth coats the greens like a dressing, wilting them, but not so much that they go limp. Albacore is a member of the tuna family with mild, meaty flesh. Pole-caught albacore is considered a "best choice" for sustainable seafood by the Monterey Bay Aquarium Seafood Watch list.

WARM ALBACORE SALAD
SERVES 4

¼ cup **extra-virgin olive oil**

¾ cup thinly sliced **yellow onion**

1 cup thinly sliced **shiitake mushrooms**

¼ pound small **red potatoes**, cut into ¼-inch dice

4 **garlic cloves**, minced

¼ cup pitted **dates**, thinly sliced

Kosher salt and freshly ground **black pepper**

¾ cup **chicken stock**

1 tablespoon chopped **preserved lemon**

1 tablespoon **curry powder**

¾ pound **albacore tuna**, cut into ¾-inch cubes

⅓ pound raw **jumbo shrimp**, chopped into ½-inch pieces

2 tablespoons dried **oregano**

½ head **napa cabbage**, finely shredded

¾ cup tightly packed finely shredded **mustard greens**

2 tablespoons **red wine vinegar**

1

Heat the oil in a large cast-iron skillet over medium heat. When the oil shimmers, add the onion, mushrooms, potatoes, garlic, and dates. Sauté until the potatoes are just tender, 7 to 9 minutes. Season with salt and pepper.

2

Stir in the stock, preserved lemon peel, and curry powder. Increase the heat to medium-high and bring to a boil, then cook for 1 minute. Add the albacore, shrimp, and oregano. Return to a boil, and cook for 2 minutes more, or until the shrimp and albacore are opaque at the middle.

3

Place the cabbage and greens in a large bowl. Pour in the hot ingredients. Add the vinegar, and toss to combine. Season with salt and pepper.

BÁNH MÌ LAMB BURGERS

IN THE MONTHS AFTER BELCAMPO OPENED, ARI TAYMOR, THE YOUNG CHEF WHOSE restaurant Alma was named best in the country by *Bon Appétit* in 2013, could often be seen at the Belcampo lunch counter on his day off. His standard order was the signature burger with a grass-fed beef patty; he called it the best in town. Another burger on the menu, the thin-patty "fast burger" that pays tribute to In-N-Out, inspired articles in the press. But of all the Belcampo burgers, the lamb burger is, if anything, the most delicious and distinctive. Lamb has the character to stand up to strong flavors, and Belcampo's repertoire tests that by mixing it with Indian chutney or, as here, with Vietnamese bánh mì layers of cucumber, jalapeño, and sour-sweet pickled vegetables.

2 cups distilled **white vinegar**

½ cup **sugar**

2 tablespoons **kosher salt**, plus more as needed

4 cups peeled and julienned **daikon radish**

3 cups peeled and julienned **carrots**

1 cup **mayonnaise**

2 tablespoons **sriracha** sauce

4 pounds **ground lamb**

Freshly ground **black pepper**

8 **seeded buns**

2 tablespoons (¼ stick) **unsalted butter**

2 **jalapeños**, sliced into ⅛-inch rounds

2 **cucumbers**, about 4 inches long, cut lengthwise into ¼-inch slices

1 cup **cilantro** leaves

Note: *The best burger is one that's been grilled outside, but these lamb burgers can also be seared in a cast-iron skillet.*

1

Combine the vinegar, sugar, and salt in a small saucepan over high heat. Bring to a boil, then remove the pan from the heat and let cool at room temperature for 10 minutes. Place the daikon and carrots in a large bowl and cover with the vinegar mixture. Marinate at room temperature for 30 minutes. Meanwhile, in a small bowl, whisk together the mayonnaise and sriracha.

2

Gently form the lamb into 8 equal-size patties; don't compress the meat any more than necessary, or it will be too tough when cooked. Generously season both sides with salt and pepper. Let the patties rest at room temperature while you fire up the grill; alternatively, heat a large cast-iron skillet over high heat. When the grill or the pan is just smoking, add the burgers, working in batches, if necessary, and sear for 3 minutes per side

for rare, 5 minutes per side for medium. Transfer to a warm plate, and let rest for 5 minutes.

3

While the burgers cook, split the buns in half. Melt the butter in a large sauté pan or griddle over high heat. Add the buns, cut-side down, and toast until golden and crisp, 2 to 3 minutes.

4

To assemble the burgers, spread sriracha mayo inside the top and bottom buns. On the bottom, layer the jalapeño, cucumber, and burger. On the top bun, layer the pickled vegetables and cilantro. Close it up and serve immediately.

MAKES 8 BURGERS

THE UNIQUE SECRET to Belcampo's burgers is the meat—Belcampo's own. To put it in geeky terms, Belcampo is a 100 percent vertically integrated meat operation, meaning that they raise their own herd on their own land, harvest the animals in their own custom-designed slaughterhouse, and sell the meat exclusively at their own butcher counters and restaurants. The result is 100 percent quality control.

POKE

***POKE* ORIGINATED IN HAWAII, BUT IT HAS SETTLED IN LA—AND NOW ALL OVER**
the country—as comfortably as sashimi did before it. The two styles play on similar themes, although to very different ends. In both, pristine raw fish is carefully cut into glistening pieces and seasoned with the distinctive but not overpowering flavors of soy sauce, sesame oil, and ginger. But poke is more robust than sashimi—it's a free-form pile of cubed fish rather than an artful arrangement of translucent slices. At Oyster Gourmet, the poke comes out with tortilla chips for a strong textural crunch.

1 pound sushi-grade **tuna** loin, such as ahi, bigeye, albacore, or blue fin

1 teaspoon **baking soda**

¼ cup minced **white onion**

3 tablespoons **soy sauce**

1 tablespoon toasted **sesame oil**

2 tablespoons toasted **sesame seeds**

1 tablespoon grated fresh **ginger**

1 teaspoon **togarashi** (Japanese chili powder)

Fried **wonton strips** or fresh **tortilla chips** (store-bought or homemade, page 78), for serving

1
Cut the tuna into in ½-inch cubes, and chill it in the refrigerator for 30 minutes. In a small bowl, dissolve the baking soda into ½ cup cold water. Add the onion, and set aside to soak for 30 minutes. Drain.

2
In a small bowl, whisk together the soy sauce, sesame oil, sesame seeds, grated ginger, togarashi, and the drained onion. The sauce can be made up to a week in advance and refrigerated in an airtight container.

3
When ready to serve, toss the cubed tuna with the sauce until well coated. Serve with fried wontons or tortillas.

SERVES 4 TO 6

THE OYSTER GOURMET'S STALL is one of the smallest at GCM—only 100 square feet—but it makes an outsize visual impact. Owner Christophe Happillon worked with architects Andrew Holder and Claus Benjamin Freyinger of the Los Angeles Design Group to style the freestanding kiosk as a dramatic oyster bar in the round. It evokes both the nautical life and the architectural history of LA.

The kiosk is made of wood with panels of stretched sailcloth canvas that can be raised or lowered with a series of ropes and pulleys, like on a boat. When lowered, the panels close as precisely as an oyster in its shell. Fully opened for business, they suggest a schooner sheeted to the wind. Architecture aficionados might also discern in the uplifted panels an oblique reference to Frank Gehry's expressive, sky-reaching design for Walt Disney Concert Hall atop Bunker Hill, a short walk from the Market.

NASHVILLE-STYLE
HOT fried CHICKEN
SANDO

HOT FRIED CHICKEN HAS BEEN A HUGE TREND IN LOS ANGELES, BUT FOR THE TEN people who haven't heard of it, it is hot, as in spicy-hot, and the level of heat can range anywhere from tingly to infernal. Generally, you want your lips to feel the burn. That said, the spice gets added after the chicken is fried, so you can adjust the intensity to taste. Either reduce the amount of cayenne in the recipe below, or make a second mild batch of coating for the fainthearted.

4 boneless, skinless **chicken breasts**

¼ teaspoon **kosher salt**

DRY DREDGE

1 cup **all-purpose flour**

2 teaspoons **garlic powder**

1 teaspoon freshly ground **black pepper**

1 teaspoon **paprika**

1 teaspoon **chicken bouillon powder**, preferably Knorr

WET DREDGE

½ cup **all-purpose flour**

½ teaspoon **kosher salt**

½ teaspoon freshly ground **black pepper**

1 **egg yolk**

¾ cup bock-style beer, preferably **Shiner Bock**

SPICY COATING

¼ cup **lard**

2 to 3 tablespoons **cayenne pepper**, to taste

1½ teaspoons **light brown sugar**

½ teaspoon freshly cracked **black pepper**

¼ teaspoon **kosher salt**

¼ teaspoon **garlic powder**

¼ teaspoon **onion powder**

⅛ teaspoon **liquid smoke**, about 6 drops

Oil, for frying

4 **hamburger buns**

Sliced **pickles**, for serving

Note: *For the best results, salt the chicken breasts a day ahead to let them "dry brine" in the refrigerator.*

1

Lay the chicken breasts out on a baking sheet and salt generously. Cover with plastic wrap and refrigerate overnight.

2

Before cooking, remove the chicken from the refrigerator and make the dredges. For the dry dredge, in a medium bowl, combine the flour, garlic powder, black pepper, paprika, and bouillon powder. Roll the chicken breasts through the dry dredge, and return them to the refrigerator, uncovered, until ready to use. In a second medium bowl, make the wet dredge by whisking together the flour, salt, black pepper, egg yolk, and beer until smooth.

3

Make the spicy coating: Melt the lard in a small saucepan over low heat. Stir in the cayenne, brown sugar, black pepper, salt, garlic powder, onion powder, and liquid smoke. Remove the pan from the heat.

4

After the chicken has rested for 1 hour, heat 2 inches of oil in a deep cast-iron skillet or Dutch oven to 325°F. Dip the chicken breasts in the wet dredge, allowing any excess to drip off, then roll them through the dry dredge again, pressing it to adhere. Shake off anything that doesn't stick, and add the chicken to the hot oil, working in batches. Fry until golden and crisp, 10 to 12 minutes per side. The internal temperature should be 165°F. While the chicken fries, reheat the spicy coating.

5

Transfer the fried chicken to a rack or a baking sheet covered with crumpled paper towels to drain. Immediately spoon the spicy coating over the top. Serve the chicken on a hamburger bun with pickles.

HORSE
THIEF BBQ

MARKET
COURT

KARAAGE IS TOKYO-STYLE FRIED CHICKEN, AND IT CAN BE SERVED AS A drinking snack, a main dish, or on a hamburger bun, maybe with a smear of wasabi mayonnaise. It's equally good whether hot, room temperature, or cold from the fridge the next day. In other words, it has all the virtues that have endeared fried chicken to people all over the world. What's distinctive about karaage is that you first season the boneless thighs with the Japanese trinity—a marinade of soy sauce, ginger, and garlic—then you coat them in a flour–potato starch (or cornstarch) mixture that fries up extra crispy. The coating is applied shake-and-bake style, and the boneless chunks take less time to fry than bone-in pieces, which makes this recipe the quickest and tidiest way to get your fried-chicken fix.

TOKYO-STYLE
KARAAGE
FRIED
CHICKEN

½ cup **soy sauce**

½ cup **sake** or **beer**

2 teaspoons **rice vinegar**

1 2-inch piece fresh **ginger**, peeled and sliced

2 **garlic cloves**, thinly sliced

2 **scallions** (white and green parts), thinly sliced

1 cup all-purpose **flour**

1 cup **potato starch** or **cornstarch**

1 tablespoon **chicken bouillon powder**, preferably Knorr

1 teaspoon **sugar**

2 pounds boneless **chicken thighs**, cut into 1½-inch pieces

Oil, for frying

Lemon wedges, for serving

Note: *The chicken needs to marinate for at least an hour, and preferably overnight, before frying. For super-crispy chicken, you can fry it a second time once it's cooled.*

1

Whisk together the soy sauce, sake, vinegar, ginger, garlic, and scallions in a large bowl or zip-top plastic bag. Add the chicken, and toss to coat. Marinate in the refrigerator for at least an hour, preferably overnight.

2

Combine the flour, potato starch, bouillon powder, and sugar in a large zip-top bag, seal, and shake to combine. Working in batches, add the chicken to the bag, and shake to coat.

3

Heat 2 inches of oil a deep cast-iron skillet or Dutch oven to 350°F. Add the coated chicken in batches, and cook until the pieces are medium brown, 6 to 8 minutes. Transfer to a paper-towel-lined tray to drain. Serve with lemon wedges alongside.

SERVES 6 TO 8

GRILLED
PORK
TOSSED WITH CELERY LEAVES

THIS SALAD OF GRILLED PORK TOSSED WITH CELERY LEAVES DOUSED IN FIERY *nahm jin* sauce has never been a regular item on the Sticky Rice menu, only an occasional special—which is too bad because it typifies the powerful flavors of Thai street food. Owner David Tewasart explains that nahm jin is also known as a seafood sauce, but he uses it at Sticky Rice as an all-purpose dipping sauce and dressing because of its perfect balance of sweet, salty, spicy, and herbaceous. The pork should ideally be grilled over charcoal, but you can also sear it in a pan. Be careful because the sugars in the marinade will want to burn.

MARINADE

Leaves from 1 bunch **cilantro**, chopped

1 teaspoon peeled and freshly grated **ginger**

1 **garlic clove**, minced

1 cup **oyster sauce**

2 tablespoons **palm sugar** or **light brown sugar**

½ teaspoon **Maggi Seasoning Sauce**

2 pounds marbled **pork**, such as neck, jowl, or shoulder, thinly sliced into 2- to 3-inch strips

NAHM JIN SAUCE

1 **garlic clove**, coarsely chopped

2 or 3 fresh **Thai chiles**, coarsely chopped

Leaves from 6 to 8 fresh **cilantro** sprigs, coarsely chopped

3 tablespoons plus 1 teaspoon **palm sugar** or **brown sugar**

¼ cup **fish sauce**

¼ cup plus 1 teaspoon freshly squeezed **lime juice**

SALAD

1 head **Chinese celery** (stems and leaves), chopped into 1-inch pieces

2 **romaine hearts**, leaves separated

½ **English cucumber**, thinly sliced

1 medium **red onion**, thinly sliced

Note: *The Chinese celery used at Sticky Rice has a stronger flavor than conventional European celery. If it's not available, substitute one heart of conventional celery, thinly sliced with leaves and all. If you happen to have a few lovage leaves, throw them in; their powerful flavor will make up the difference.*

1

In a large bowl, whisk together the cilantro, ginger, garlic, oyster sauce, palm sugar, and seasoning sauce. Add the pork and toss to coat. Cover and marinate at room temperature for an hour, or refrigerate for up to 12 hours.

2

Make the nahm jin sauce: Grind together the garlic, chiles, and cilantro in a mortar or pulse in a blender or food processor until well combined but not pureed. Incorporate the palm sugar slowly so it dissolves. Add the fish sauce and lime juice. When all the ingredients are blended, the sauce should be bright green. Taste and adjust the seasonings, if needed.

3

Heat a grill or preheat the broiler. Add the marinated pork and cook until cooked through, about 5 minutes per side.

4

Meanwhile, make the salad: In a large bowl, combine the Chinese celery, romaine, cucumber, and onion. Add the nahm jin, a few tablespoons at a time, and toss to coat. Add the pork, and toss to combine, drizzling in more nahm jin if necessary. Serve immediately.

SERVES 6 TO 8

DON'T BE MISLED BY THE NAME OF THIS DISH. THAI BBQ CHICKEN DOESN'T HAVE anything in common with American BBQ chicken, except, perhaps, that both are best grilled over a fire. The coconut milk marinade here is pungent with garlic, cilantro, white pepper, and fish sauce, which provides salt, umami, and the seaside funk that helps define Thai cooking. Turmeric tints the chicken a fetching yellow. Sticky Rice owner David Tewasart explains that Thai cuisine often adds a second wave of flavor to grilled meat with a dipping sauce. At GCM, Thai BBQ Chicken is served with Sticky Rice (page 130) and a ramekin of sweet-and-sour *nam jihm gai*. (The dipping sauce is also great with crudités or used as a dressing for a quick cucumber salad.)

thai BBQ CHICKEN

1 cup full-fat canned **coconut milk**

1 teaspoon grated fresh **turmeric** or ground turmeric

2 tablespoons minced **garlic**

2 tablespoons minced **cilantro roots** (or ¼ cup minced leaves and stems)

¼ cup **fish sauce**

1 teaspoon ground **white pepper**

2 pounds boneless **chicken breasts**

Nam jihm gai (recipe below)

Note: *The chicken needs to marinate for at least an hour. At Sticky Rice, the chefs vacuum-seal it with the marinade the day before and store it in the refrigerator overnight. And while nothing beats cooking on a grill, this recipe can also be prepared in the kitchen using the broiler.*

1

In a large bowl, whisk together the coconut milk, turmeric, garlic, cilantro, fish sauce, and white pepper. Add the chicken and turn to coat, massaging the marinade into every nook and cranny.

Cover the bowl with plastic wrap, and place in the refrigerator to marinate for at least an hour, preferably overnight.

2

Heat the grill or preheat the broiler. Grill or broil the chicken until cooked through, 8 to 10 minutes per side, letting the edges char for the best flavor.

3

Serve with ramekins of nam jihm gai dipping sauce alongside.

SERVES 6 TO 8

NAM JIHM GAI
(SWEET-AND-SOUR DIPPING SAUCE)

MAKES ABOUT 1 CUP

½ cup **sambal oelek**

⅓ cup **garlic cloves**

½ cup **white vinegar**

⅓ cup plus 1 tablespoon **sugar**

2 teaspoons **salt**

1

Combine the sambal oelek, garlic, and vinegar in a blender or food processor, and pulse until smooth.

2

Transfer the mixture to a small saucepan and bring to a boil over high heat. Reduce the heat to medium, and add the sugar and salt. Simmer until the sauce has reduced by one-quarter, 10 to 15 minutes. Remove the pan from the heat, and set aside until cool. Store refrigerated in an airtight container for up to 3 days.

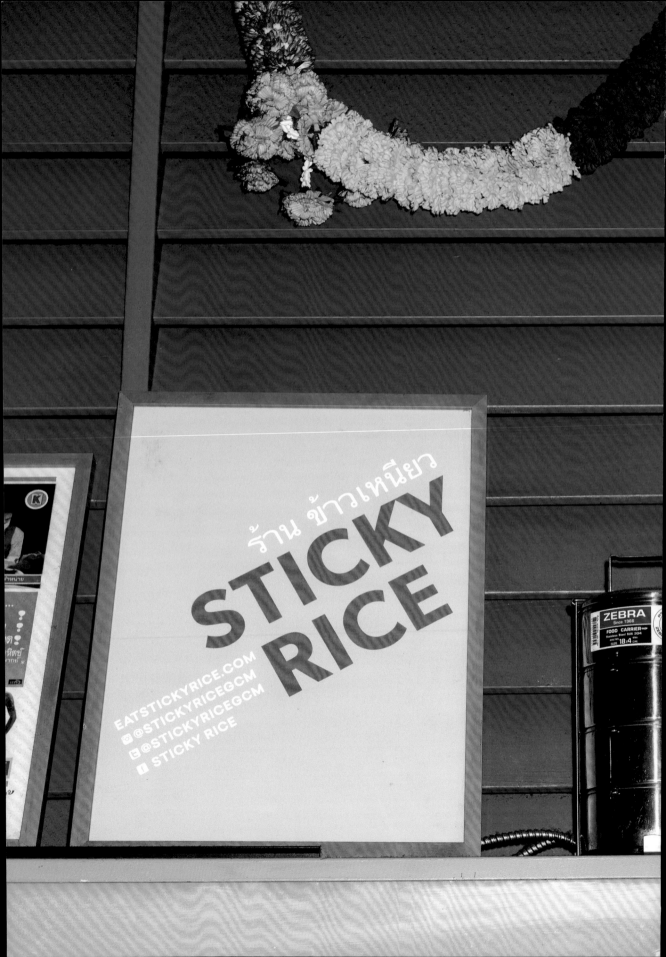

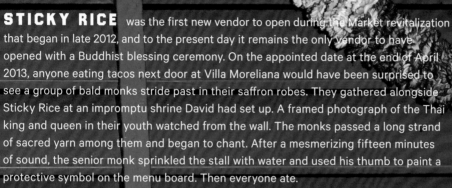

STICKY RICE was the first new vendor to open during the Market revitalization that began in late 2012, and to the present day it remains the only vendor to have opened with a Buddhist blessing ceremony. On the appointed date at the end of April 2013, anyone eating tacos next door at Villa Moreliana would have been surprised to see a group of bald monks stride past in their saffron robes. They gathered alongside Sticky Rice at an impromptu shrine David had set up. A framed photograph of the Thai king and queen in their youth watched from the wall. The monks passed a long strand of sacred yarn among them and began to chant. After a mesmerizing fifteen minutes of sound, the senior monk sprinkled the stall with water and used his thumb to paint a protective symbol on the menu board. Then everyone ate.

Apparently the blessings worked. Business grew steadily month by month. In time, David remodeled the stall to evoke the famous Bangkok night markets. He eventually expanded into an adjacent stall to open Sticky Rice II, which serves noodles. (To read more about how Sticky Rice got to the Market in the first place, see page 29.)

BIG MEATBALLS

WITH AMATRICIANA SAUCE

SERVES 5

CHEF BRUCE KALMAN IS A BIG GUY, AND HIS SPECIALTY IS BIG FLAVORS. EVEN seemingly simple dishes—like his signature *spaghetti alla chitarra*—come out of the kitchen with a focus and intensity of flavor that's hard to figure out. This recipe for pork meatballs reveals a few of his secrets. It achieves depth and complexity thanks to a fistful of grated Parmigiano-Reggiano and another of chopped smoked bacon. The amatriciana sauce brings in the bright clarity of tomatoes at their most essential. Serving the meatballs draped with slices of lardo, Italian cured fatback, is a classic Bruce move—and a spectacular culinary example of gilding the lily.

Oil, for the baking sheet

MEATBALLS

6½ ounces smoked **bacon**, ground or very finely minced

½ cup grated **Parmigiano-Reggiano cheese**

¼ cup **ricotta cheese**

2 **eggs**

1 tablespoon chopped fresh flat-leaf **parsley**

2 tablespoons chopped fresh **oregano**

1 tablespoon minced **garlic**

4 teaspoons **kosher salt**

1 teaspoon freshly ground **black pepper**

2 teaspoons dried **red chile flakes**

½ cup dried **bread crumbs**

¼ cup **filtered water**

1½ pounds ground **pork shoulder**

AMATRICIANA SAUCE

2 tablespoons **extra-virgin olive oil**

4 ounces smoked **bacon**, chopped

6 large whole fresh **basil** leaves

½ teaspoon dried **red chile flakes**

½ large **red onion**, julienned

4 **garlic cloves**, smashed

2 28-ounce cans whole **San Marzano tomatoes**, drained and crushed

Kosher salt and freshly ground **black pepper**

FOR SERVING

5 ¾-inch-thick slices of **sourdough bread**

1 **garlic clove**, peeled

3 tablespoons thinly sliced **caper berries**

¼ cup grated **Parmigiano-Reggiano cheese**

10 thin slices **lardo** (optional)

 1

Preheat the oven to 400°F. Lightly oil a baking sheet.

2

Make the meatballs: Place all the meatball ingredients except the pork in a large bowl. Using your hands, mix until thoroughly combined. Gently fold in the pork just until integrated—don't overmix. Form the mixture into 10 big meatballs using a 3-ounce ice cream scoop as a guide, and place them on the prepared baking sheet. Transfer to the oven and bake until well browned and cooked through, 25 to 35 minutes.

3

While the meatballs bake, make the amatriciana sauce: Combine the olive oil and the bacon in a large saucepan over

medium heat. Cook until the fat is rendered, 8 to 10 minutes. Add the basil and chile flakes, and cook for 1 minute more. Add the onion and garlic, and season to taste with salt and pepper. Cook for 15 minutes, or until the onions are lightly caramelized. Add the tomatoes, increase the heat to medium-high to maintain a lively simmer, and cook for 10 minutes. Remove the pan from the heat. Taste and adjust the seasonings, if needed.

4

Transfer the cooked meatballs into the sauce, and keep hot over low heat until ready to serve.

5

Preheat the broiler. Toast one side of the sourdough bread under the broiler until well browned, and, while still hot, rub lightly with the garlic clove. Transfer the meatballs to a large serving platter, and spoon the sauce over them. Top with the sliced caper berries and grated Parmigiano-Reggiano. Top each meatball with a slice of lardo, if using. Serve with the toast alongside.

FOR THIS GUTSY TAKE ON CURRIED SHRIMP, PRAWN CHEF MARK PEEL MARINATES jumbo shrimp in curry powder, then simmers them in broth and cream along with diced potatoes and sautéed Japanese winter squash. A spoonful of chili paste punches up the flavor; a sprinkle of peanuts adds crunch. Served over a bowl of warm rice, as it's done at Prawn, the dish takes on an element of comfort food; you could also spoon it over polenta for an unexpected riff on shrimp and grits. For a different approach, pair Curried Shrimp with dressy vegetable sides—maybe a frisée-citrus salad—as the main dish for a sit-down dinner party.

1 pound raw jumbo **shrimp**

¼ cup plus 2 tablespoons best-quality **curry powder**

⅓ cup **extra-virgin olive oil**

1 small **yellow onion**, thinly sliced

1½ cups (¼-inch dice) small **red potatoes**

1 cup (¼-inch dice) peeled **kabocha squash**

Kosher salt and freshly ground **black pepper**

1 cup **chicken broth**

1 cup **heavy cream**

2 tablespoons **sambal oelek chili paste**

⅓ cup roasted unsalted **peanuts**, chopped

2 tablespoons chopped fresh **parsley**

Cooked **rice**, for serving

1

In a large bowl, toss the shrimp with ¼ cup of the curry powder, and let marinate, covered, in the refrigerator for 1 hour.

2

Heat the olive oil in a large skillet over high heat. When the oil shimmers, add the onion, potatoes, and squash. Season with salt and pepper. Sauté until tender, 6 to 8 minutes.

3

Stir in the broth, cream, chili paste, and the remaining 2 tablespoons curry powder. Bring to a boil, and cook for 3 minutes. Add the shrimp and peanuts, then return to a boil and cook until the shrimp are pink and opaque, 3 to 5 minutes. Season with salt and pepper. Garnish with the chopped parsley, and serve over rice.

SERVES 4

CURRIED
SHRIMP
★ ★ ★

PRAWN CHEF MARK PEEL was a legend on the LA fine dining scene long before he opened his stall at GCM. He got his early training at Chez Panisse in Berkeley and then honed his chops as Wolfgang Puck's right hand at Spago in Beverly Hills. That's also where Mark met pastry chef extraordinaire Nancy Silverton. They married, cofounded La Brea Bakery, and in 1989 opened Campanile, a landmark of California cooking that helped redefine fine dining in Los Angeles. Campanile's menu offered a sophisticated take on rustic cuisine, and the dining room combined elegant service with an easygoing atmosphere. The restaurant helped establish a now familiar culinary template with its focus on seasonal menus, local farmers, an open kitchen, live-fire cooking, house-baked breads, and homemade charcuterie. Mark and Nancy eventually divorced, but Campanile continued its long run until late 2012, and its legacy can still be found in the dozens of LA chefs who trained there.

When GCM first approached Mark about doing a new project in DTLA, he explained that he wanted to put his fine dining skills—and his fine dining ideals—to use for a more democratic audience. He was also passionate about supporting healthy oceans and well-regulated fisheries. Put it all together, and Mark came up with Prawn. (The original name, Bombo, had to be changed after it was discovered that a restaurant in North Carolina had filed a trademark application for "Bombo" *one day* before Mark submitted his.) Mark describes Prawn as "chef-casual sustainable seafood," with a focus on healthy steamed, stewed, and braised dishes prepared in steam kettles. We call it a great second act from one of LA's homegrown master chefs.

VALERIA'S

STALL

D - G

THE WORD *POSOLE* REFERS TO BOTH THE PRINCIPAL INGREDIENT—DRIED HOMINY corn—and the end result of this recipe, a robust stew of pork and cooked hominy in a staining red broth. The hominy kernels "blossom" and split open during cooking in the same way that popcorn pops, although in less dramatic fashion. Posole is a wonderful cold-weather meal. Because it is inevitably cooked in a large batch, making posole also is a good excuse to invite friends over. Or you can freeze what you don't eat right away, and you'll have an extra meal stashed away for the next cold or rainy day.

posole ROJO

SERVES 20

3 pounds dried **posole**, rinsed and drained

6 pounds **pork shoulder**, cut into 1-inch cubes

4 pounds **pork bones**

2 **pig's feet**, split

3 medium **yellow onions**, chopped

3 small heads of **garlic**, halved crosswise

8 fresh **thyme** sprigs

8 dried **bay leaves**

1 tablespoon dried **oregano**

6 tablespoons **chicken bouillon powder**, preferably Knorr

1 pound whole dried **guajillo chiles**

Kosher salt and freshly ground **black pepper**

GARNISHES

1 small head of **cabbage**, shredded

4 bunches of **radishes**, thinly sliced

Red Salsa (page 82)

5 **limes**, quartered

2 medium **white onions**, diced and soaked in cold water for 30 minutes

Dried **Mexican oregano**

Tostadas, for serving

Note: *Posole takes hours and hours on the stove, almost a whole day. The best strategy is to cook it in advance, then refrigerate overnight. The next day, the fat will have hardened, making it easy to skim and discard. As with many stews, the flavor of posole only improves with a night of rest.*

1

In a large pot, cover the posole with 3 quarts water. Bring to a boil over high heat, then reduce the heat to low and simmer for 2 to 3 hours, until the skins loosen. Turn off the heat, and allow the mixture to cool. Drain, and vigorously rub the kernels between your palms to remove the skins and the little nub where the kernel attaches to the cob.

2

Bring another 3 quarts water to a boil in a large stockpot over high heat. Add the posole, and cook for 30 minutes. Add the pork meat, bones, and feet. Then add the onions, garlic, herbs, and bouillon powder. Return to a boil, then reduce the heat to medium and simmer. Skim the scum that rises to the surface.

3

Meanwhile, in a large cast-iron skillet over high heat, toast the guajillo chiles until fragrant, about 3 minutes per side. Remove them from the pan to cool, then remove and discard the stems. Transfer the chiles to a small

saucepan. Add just enough water to cover and a few pinches of salt. Bring to a boil over high heat, then reduce the heat to low and simmer, partially covered, for 20 minutes, or until softened. Reserve a cup of the cooking liquid, then drain the chiles. Transfer to a blender or food processor and pulse, adding cooking liquid, 1 tablespoon at a time, to make a thick salsa. Add the salsa to the posole. Simmer the posole for 4 hours. Season with salt and pepper.

4

When the posole is done, remove the pig's feet with a slotted spoon, and transfer them to a cutting board to cool. Using tongs or your fingers, pick off the succulent skin and bits of meat, and chop them finely; discard the bones. Stir the pig skin and meat into the posole. Turn off the heat, and let the posole cool for about an hour, then refrigerate overnight.

5

Before serving, skim the fat off the chilled posole and discard. Warm the posole over medium heat for 1 hour.

6

Ladle the posole into bowls. Serve with the shredded cabbage, sliced radishes, salsa, lime wedges, diced onion, oregano, and tostadas.

CARNE GUISADA

CARNE GUISADA SIMPLY MEANS STEWED MEAT, AND THE BASIC OUTLINE OF THIS recipe from Sarita's Pupuseria will be familiar to anyone who's ever made American-style beef stew. First you brown the meat, then simmer it with potatoes and vegetables until tender. The result is everything you need for a satisfying meal—some protein, some carbs, and some tender veggies, all sauced with liquid comfort. What makes this stew distinctly Salvadoran is the spice-garlic paste achiote. Then there's also chef-owner Sara Clark's trick for making the sauce: You first puree the raw onion, garlic, tomato, and bell pepper with a cup of water, then pour the liquefied aromatics over the meat. As the sauce cooks down, the pureed vegetables give the stew body as well as flavor. If you'd like stronger seasonings, stir in an extra tablespoon of achiote toward the end of cooking, when you add the olives.

¼ cup **extra-virgin olive oil**

3¼ pounds **chuck roast**, cut into 1-inch cubes

1 tablespoon **Worcestershire sauce**

1 tablespoon **Achiote Paste** (page 105)

1 tablespoon prepared **yellow mustard**

1 tablespoon **beef bouillon powder**

2 tablespoons dried **oregano**

2 dried **bay leaves**

2 pounds **Roma tomatoes**, quartered

½ medium **yellow onion**, coarsely chopped

½ **green bell pepper**, stem and seeds removed

7 **garlic cloves**

1 pound **Yukon Gold potatoes**, cubed

2 medium **carrots**, sliced

½ pound **green beans**, trimmed

Kosher salt and freshly ground **black pepper**

½ cup whole **green** or **black olives**, pitted

1
Heat the olive oil over medium-high heat in a large skillet. When the oil shimmers, add the meat, working in batches if necessary, and sear until browned, 5 minutes per side.

2
While the meat browns, in a small bowl, whisk together the Worcestershire, achiote, mustard, bouillon powder, and oregano. Stir the mixture into the meat as it cooks, and add the bay leaves. Lower the heat and continue to cook until the meat forms a nice crust, about 10 minutes more.

3
In a blender or food processor, combine the tomatoes, onion, bell pepper, garlic, and 1 cup water. Pulse until smooth, then pour the mixture over the meat. Bring to a boil, then cover and reduce the heat to low. Simmer until the meat begins to tenderize, about 30 to 45 minutes.

4
Add the potatoes, carrots, and green beans to the pot. Simmer for 20 minutes more, or until the vegetables are just tender. Season with salt and pepper. Stir in the olives, warm through, and serve.

SERVES 8

VELVET STEAK
WITH CHIMICHURRI

REGULAR CUSTOMERS AT BELCAMPO KNOW TO ASK THE BUTCHER FOR recommendations; often some unfamiliar cut is tucked between the strip steaks and rib roasts in the case. These are the odd bits—velvet steaks, hanger steaks, bavettes—that don't show up at grocery stores, or cuts that are overlooked because their small quantities don't fit the production needs of Big Beef. They're also some of the tastiest pieces, sometimes called "butcher's cuts" because the butcher might take them home for herself.

A good cut of beef doesn't require a fancy sauce. Belcampo's recommended accompaniment for any sort of steak is this chimichurri, a simple South American sauce of chopped herbs, olive oil, and vinegar. Think of it as a dressing, which means the exact combination of ingredients can vary quite a bit, so don't worry if you're missing one or two elements. As always, let the steak rest for 10 minutes or more before you slice it.

1½ cups packed fresh **flat-leaf parsley** leaves

4 **garlic cloves**, coarsely chopped

2 tablespoons packed fresh **oregano** leaves

1½ tablespoons packed fresh **rosemary** leaves

1 tablespoon packed fresh **thyme** leaves

1 fresh **bay leaf**

1 teaspoon dried **red chile flakes**

¾ cup **extra-virgin olive oil**

⅓ cup **sherry vinegar**

Kosher salt and freshly ground **black pepper**

3 pounds **velvet steak**, **bavette**, or **hanger steak**

Note: *This sauce is great on any steak, whatever part of the cow it comes from. Chimichurri adds succulence to lean cuts and balances the richness of fatty cuts such as rib eye. The sauce will keep in the refrigerator for up to 2 days; let it come to room temperature before serving.*

1

In a blender or food processor, combine the parsley, garlic, oregano, rosemary, thyme, bay leaf, and chile flakes. Pulse until the herbs are finely chopped. With the motor running, stream in the olive oil and vinegar. Season with salt and black pepper, and transfer to a small bowl; you'll have about 1½ cups. Let stand at room temperature for at least 1 hour before serving.

2

Heat the grill or a cast-iron skillet over high heat. Sear the steak for 5 minutes per side for medium-rare, or to your preferred doneness. Transfer to a platter and let rest for 10 minutes. Slice the steak against the grain, and drizzle with chimichurri sauce. Serve with extra sauce on the side.

SERVES 6 TO 8

PORK BELLY

WITH APPLE FENNEL SLAW

HORSE THIEF BBQ HANGS ITS HAT ON TEXAS-STYLE DRY-RUB BRISKET SLOW-
cooked with wood smoke. So why isn't that recipe here? Mainly because it's impossible to duplicate at home. Smoked brisket is not a home-kitchen project, unless you have a smoker and a pile of split oak firewood in your home kitchen. This recipe for slow-cooked pork belly, on the other hand, does catch the spirit, if not the letter, of BBQ law in the oven, thanks to the combination of a dark dry-rub spice mix and an extended braise in malty, toasty bock-style beer. The fresh slaw of apples and fennel works as a refreshing counterpoint to the rich pork.

1 cup packed **light brown sugar**

1 cup **sweet paprika**

10 tablespoons **kosher salt**

10 tablespoons coarsely ground **black pepper**

3 tablespoons **mustard powder**

3 tablespoons **chili powder**

6 tablespoons **garlic powder**

6 tablespoons **onion powder**

2 pounds unsmoked **pork belly**, skin removed

2 tablespoons **extra-virgin olive oil**

1 12-ounce bottle **bock-style beer**, preferably Shiner Bock

SLAW

2 tablespoons **fennel seeds**

⅔ cup **honey**

5 tablespoons **apple cider vinegar**

1 small **napa cabbage**, shredded

1 **Granny Smith apple**, cored and sliced into matchsticks

1 large **fennel** bulb, thinly sliced on a mandoline

¼ cup chopped fresh **mint**

¼ cup chopped fresh **basil**

Kosher salt and freshly ground **black pepper**

1

Preheat the oven to 350°F. In a large bowl, combine the brown sugar, paprika, salt, pepper, mustard powder, chili powder, garlic powder, and onion powder. Rub the mixture into the pork belly on all sides.

2

Heat the olive oil in a large Dutch oven over high heat. When the oil shimmers, add the pork, fat-side down, and sear until browned, about 10 minutes. Turn the pork over, and pour in the beer. Bring the mixture to a boil, then transfer the pan to the oven. Cook uncovered until the internal temperature reaches 195°F, 1½ to 2 hours. (Alternatively, smoke the dry-rubbed meat in a smoker at 250°F for 4 hours.)

3

While the pork cooks, make the slaw: Toast the fennel seeds in a small sauté pan over medium heat until fragrant, about 5 minutes. Add the honey, which will boil up. Reduce the heat to low, and simmer for 2 minutes. Strain the mixture through a fine-mesh sieve set over a small bowl, discarding the fennel seeds. Add the vinegar to the honey and whisk to combine. Taste and adjust the seasonings. In a large bowl, combine the cabbage, apple, fennel, mint, and basil. Pour the dressing over the slaw, and toss to coat. Season with salt and pepper.

SERVES 8

VEG

TORRES PRODUCE CARRIES FRUITS AND VEGETABLES THAT YOU CAN'T FIND MOST places, stuff that even food experts have to look up. There's purslane (*verdolagas* in Spanish), mirlitons (chayote), and Mexican hawthorne (*tejocotes*). This recipe from Torres uses a more familiar salad bowl of ingredients but puts them together with an unmistakably Mexican lime-cilantro flavor profile. Chopping everything together melds the flavors—and also makes Adele happy. She loves chopped salads and always asks for hers to be double-chopped, sometimes even triple-chopped. This recipe can be adapted to include other vegetables (radishes!), as well as protein (shredded chicken or garbanzo beans), and crumbled cotija cheese (feta can be substituted).

ENSALADA
mixta
(CHOPPED)
SALAD

1 tablespoon **baking soda**

1 small **red onion**, sliced as thinly as possible

2 **Persian cucumbers**, cut into ¼-inch dice

2 **Roma tomatoes**, seeded and cut into ¼-inch dice

½ cup chopped fresh **cilantro** leaves, minced

1 medium head of **iceberg lettuce**, shredded

3 **avocados**, cut into chunks

Juice of 3 **limes** or small **lemons** (about ¼ cup)

¼ teaspoon **kosher salt**

Freshly ground **black pepper**

1

In a small bowl, dissolve the baking soda in 1 cup water. Add the onion and let soak for 15 minutes to mellow its strong taste. Drain and rinse the onion with fresh water. Transfer the onion to a large bowl and add the cucumbers, tomatoes, cilantro, lettuce, and avocados. Toss to combine. Turn the mixture onto a cutting board, and chop it all together with several passes of a large chef's knife or mezzaluna.

2

Return the chopped ingredients to the bowl. Dress with the citrus juice, salt, and pepper to taste. Serve immediately.

SERVES 4 TO 6

THE MOTTO AT MADCAPRA, THE NOT-QUITE-TRADITIONAL FALAFEL STAND FROM chefs Sara Kramer and Sarah Hymanson, is "Because vegetables." But the Sara(h)s, as they are known around the Market, insist Madcapra is *not* a vegetarian restaurant. Because, sometimes, grilled lamb. They serve this tomato salad as a side with falafel sandwiches, but at home it would go equally well with any grilled or roasted meat. The dressing gets a kick from chili oil, and the cardamom note is a brilliant inspiration. It's one of those flavor pairings that, once you try it, you'll wonder why the idea never occurred to you before.

3 dried **chiles de árbol** or 1 dried **cayenne pepper**

2 tablespoons whole **black peppercorns**

12 green **cardamom pods**

¼ cup **extra-virgin olive oil**

2 **garlic cloves**, grated

2 pounds **tomatoes** of varying sizes, shapes, and colors, cut into irregular chunks

1 pint **cherry tomatoes** in varying colors, halved

1 **lemon**, halved

¼ teaspoon fine **sea salt**

2 tablespoons toasted **sesame seeds**

1 bunch **cilantro**, leaves coarsely chopped

Labneh and good crusty **bread**, for serving

Note: You can make the spice oil the day ahead and store it in the fridge. Bring it to room temperature for an hour before using.

1

Make the spice oil: Heat a small skillet over medium heat. When the pan is hot, add the chiles, peppercorns, and cardamom, and toast until fragrant, 2 to 3 minutes. Transfer the spices to a small bowl to cool. Grind the toasted spices in a mortar, spice grinder, or food processor—but not too fine. Combine the oil and the garlic in a small bowl, then whisk in the spices.

2

Combine the tomatoes in a large bowl with half the spice oil, the juice of half a lemon, and the salt. Mix gently to avoid damaging the tomatoes. Taste and add some or all of the remaining spice oil and lemon juice to taste. Garnish with the sesame seeds and cilantro. Serve with labneh and bread alongside.

SERVES 6 TO 8

TOMATO SALAD WITH CHILE, BLACK PEPPER & CARDAMOM

PRESSED CUCUMBER SALAD

RAMEN HOOD CHEF RAHUL KHOPKAR'S RÉSUMÉ INCLUDES A STINT AT NOMA IN Copenhagen, a perennial contender for the title of world's best restaurant. This cucumber salad, a popular side dish with Ramen Hood's vegan ramen, uses a neat trick borrowed from that world of high-end modernist cuisine. Rahul seals the cucumbers in a vacuum bag overnight, transforming them into translucent chunks, almost like polished jade. Unfortunately, there's no way to reproduce the effect without a vacuum sealer. (In the home kitchen, vacuum sealers are typically used to package food for freezing.) But even without one, it's still well worth making this salad with regular sliced cucumbers because of the sweet-and-spicy dressing and the fried garbanzo beans, which deliver a crouton-like crunch.

2 pounds **Persian cucumbers** (10 to 12)

⅓ cup **rice vinegar**

⅔ cup **toasted sesame oil**

⅓ cup **light brown sugar**

½ teaspoon **kosher salt**, plus more as needed

Oil, for frying

½ cup canned **chickpeas**, rinsed, drained, and dried on paper towels

2 **avocados**, cut into chunks

1 tablespoon **sesame seeds**, toasted

½ teaspoon **Korean red chile flakes** (gochugaru) or **Aleppo chile flakes**

Note: *The dressing can be made the day before and stored refrigerated in an airtight container. If you're using a vacuum sealer, the cucumbers marinate overnight.*

1

Peel the cucumbers, and slice them into irregular ¾-inch chunks. Vacuum-seal them in a bag, and refrigerate overnight.

2

In a small bowl, whisk together the vinegar, sesame oil, brown sugar, and salt. Taste and adjust the seasoning, if needed. The noticeable sweetness will complement the vinegar's acidity and make the dressing pop.

3

Fry the chickpeas: Heat 1 inch of oil to 350°F in a small saucepan. Working in batches, fry the chickpeas until crispy, 2 to 3 minutes. Using a slotted spoon, transfer them to a paper-towel-lined tray to drain. Season with a pinch of salt.

4

Immediately before serving, place the cucumbers in a large bowl and season with 2 pinches of salt. Add the avocado. Add the dressing, ¼ cup at a time, and toss to coat. Add the toasted sesame seeds and chile flakes, and toss to distribute. Garnish with the fried chickpeas.

SERVES 6 TO 8

RADICCHIO SALAD

SALADS HOLD A SPECIAL APPEAL FOR ADELE AND THE REST OF THE GCM TEAM, who eat at the Market almost every day and sometimes need a break from carne asada, pastrami, and smoked brisket. This example from chef Chris Feldmeier instantly became a team favorite when Bar Moruno opened near the Hill Street entrance. Chris's menu was Spanish-inspired, although, strictly speaking, this salad is not anything you'd find in Seville; the Spanish touch comes in subtly with the marinated white anchovies, which are milder and far less salty than the usual variety. The surprise ingredient is fermented pickles, while the fresh dill and chives in the yogurt dressing bring it all together. Although Moruno closed, Chris's gone-but-not-forgotten Market classic is a piece of Market history you can make at home.

DRESSING

2 cups full-fat plain **Greek yogurt**

½ cup finely chopped fermented **cucumber pickles**, such as kosher dills (see Note)

1 tablespoon **pickle brine**, plus more as needed

4 **garlic cloves**, grated

¼ cup chopped fresh **dill**

4 tablespoons minced fresh **chives**

1 tablespoon freshly squeezed **lemon juice**, plus more as needed

1 to 2 tablespoons **extra-virgin olive oil**

SALAD

3 large heads **radicchio**, leaves rinsed and patted dry

2 hard-boiled **eggs**, peeled and sliced

3 fresh **dill** sprigs, fronds only

16 **white anchovies**

½ cup (½-inch slices) fermented **pickles** (see Note)

Note: Be sure to use fermented pickles, such as the Deli Dills from Wexler's on page 148, rather than vinegar pickles, which will throw the salad out of balance.

1

Make the dressing: In a medium bowl, whisk together the yogurt, chopped pickles, pickle brine, garlic, chopped dill, 2 tablespoons of the chives, and the lemon juice. Taste and adjust with more pickle brine or lemon juice, as needed. Slowly stream in the olive oil to taste, whisking constantly to emulsify.

2

Place half the radicchio leaves in a large bowl. Add the dressing, and massage it into the leaves with your hands until the radicchio is thoroughly coated. Add the remaining radicchio, and toss to combine.

3

Assemble the salad: Cover the bottom of a salad bowl or serving platter with a thick layer of coated radicchio. Strew it with half the eggs, picked dill, anchovies, sliced pickles, and 1 tablespoon of the chives. Add another layer of radicchio, and garnish with the remaining eggs, dill, chives, anchovies, and pickles. Serve immediately.

SERVES 4

CALIFORNIA IS AMERICA'S SALAD BOWL, BUT DROUGHT IS A FACT OF THE
California climate, and changes related to global warming have made the state's annual
rainfall even less predictable. Because lettuce is a thirsty crop, GCM produce vendor District
Market came up with a "drought salad" to showcase vegetables that consume less water.
Root vegetables, growing underground as they do, fit the bill, because they lose less water
through evaporation than leafy lettuce. Baby spinach takes less water simply because it's
harvested sooner than mature spinach leaves.

DROUGHT SALAD

½ cup **apple cider vinegar**

¼ cup **apple cider**

⅓ cup **extra-virgin olive oil**

1 tablespoon **Dijon mustard**

2 tablespoons **pale honey**

1 teaspoon **kosher salt**

½ teaspoon freshly ground **black
pepper**

Pinch of dried **thyme**

1 **shallot**, thinly sliced

1 **garlic clove**, lightly crushed

5 medium **red** or **golden beets**,
peeled and julienned

3 medium **carrots**, grated

½ small **jicama**, julienned

2 cups canned or home-cooked
black-eyed peas

7 cups **baby spinach** leaves

½ cup fresh **flat-leaf parsley** leaves

½ cup crumbled **chèvre**

1

Whisk together the vinegar,
cider, olive oil, mustard, honey,
salt, pepper, and thyme in a small
bowl. Add the shallot and garlic,
and stir to combine. Let rest at
room temperature for 30 minutes
for the flavors to meld. Discard
the clove of garlic before serving.

2

In a large serving bowl, toss
together the beets, carrots,
jicama, black-eyed peas, spinach,
parsley, and chèvre. Pour the
dressing over top, and toss to
coat.

SERVES 8

AS AT MOST THAI RESTAURANTS, *SOM TUM* (GREEN PAPAYA SALAD) IS A STAPLE at Sticky Rice. Owner David Tewasart explains that in Thailand, som tum is traditionally pounded together in a large clay mortar, called a *pok pok*, named for the sound it makes when used. That's the way they do it at Sticky Rice, too, and one cook spends most of the day working the pok pok, because every som tum is made to order. At home, you can get by without a pok pok by pounding the ingredients with your fists in a large bowl—a good activity for releasing stress, as well. Sticky Rice's chefs also have particular way to julienne the main ingredient: Hold a peeled green papaya in one hand, stem up, and lightly chop into it with a knife at ¼-inch intervals, then shave the surface to make the julienne.

2 fresh **Thai chiles**, thinly sliced

8 **garlic cloves**, coarsely chopped

2 teaspoons freshly squeezed **lime juice**

2 teaspoons finely chopped **palm sugar** or **turbinado sugar**

2 tablespoons **fish sauce**, or to taste

10 **cherry tomatoes**, halved

½ cup (1-inch pieces) **Chinese long beans** or fresh **green beans**

1 small **green papaya** (1 to 1½ pounds), peeled and shredded or grated

¼ cup **peanuts**, toasted and chopped

Notes: *Som tum is best made in small batches. If you need more than this recipe makes, you'll have better results if you make two batches rather than doubling the specified quantities*

Chinese long beans, which look like rough-skinned green beans that forgot to stop growing until almost 2 feet in length, are available at Asian markets and many California farmer's markets. Regular green beans could be substituted.

1

In a mortar and pestle (or in a medium bowl with a wooden spoon), crush the chiles, garlic, lime juice, palm sugar, and fish sauce until the sugar dissolves. Add the tomatoes and long beans, and bruise them.

2

If your mortar is large enough, add the green papaya and mix the salad, alternating between a pounding motion and turning the mixture with a spoon. If not, combine the papaya and the other ingredients in a large bowl, and use your hands to pound and mix it.

3

Transfer the salad to a serving platter, and drizzle it with the liquid from the mortar or bowl. Garnish with the peanuts. Serve immediately.

SERVES 2 TO 3

SOM TUM
(GREEN PAPAYA SALAD)

CURRYWURST, GERMANY'S MOST POPULAR STREET FOOD, IS A SAUSAGE splashed with a curry-ketchup sauce. It's typically served sliced on a plate instead of on a bun, and at Berlin Currywurst, the "cutlery" offered is a little wooden fork thingy, which is just large enough make fast work of the sauerkraut salad alongside. A splash of pineapple juice in the dressing is unexpected, even slightly exotic. Even if you're not making currywurst, the sauerkraut salad would be a great side dish alongside any kind of sausage, including hot dogs.

1 pound **sauerkraut** (2 cups tightly packed), rinsed and drained

2 **scallions** (white and green parts), chopped

½ medium **yellow onion**, grated (about ⅓ cup)

2 medium **carrots**, grated

1 large **orange**, sectioned and chopped

¼ cup **white wine vinegar**

⅓ cup **pineapple juice**

¼ cup **vegetable oil**

½ teaspoon fine **sea salt**

1 teaspoon freshly ground **black pepper**

1
Squeeze out any excess moisture from the sauerkraut. Place it in a large bowl along with the scallions, onion, carrot, and orange.

2
In a small bowl, whisk together the vinegar, pineapple juice, oil, salt, and pepper. Taste and adjust the seasonings, if needed. Pour the dressing over the sauerkraut mixture, and toss to coat.

SERVES 6 TO 8

WHAT YOU LEARN from talking to Berlin Currywurst co-owner Hardeep Manak is that currywurst—basically, a hot dog—is more than what you might think. The idea of selling sausage with a spicy ketchup-curry condiment first appeared at the end of World War II, when out-of-work Berliners sold currywurst from street stalls to survive. In a sense, those street vendors were precursors to the pop-up stalls and food trucks that have helped define LA cooking since 2009. In both cases, economic necessity gave rise to popular and long-lasting culinary inventions.

"Currywurst is the history of entrepreneurship," says Hardeep, making the obvious point that he and his wife/business partner, Lena Manak, put their spin on the same entrepreneurial spirit. "We took this street food and gave it high-quality ingredients and brought in design and music."

Hardeep adds that while Berlin Currywurst is a food stall, it's also his way to introduce people to the history of his home country.

"For us, Berlin Currywurst is a way to talk about German culture and Berlin youth culture today," he says. "The education part of talking to customers is way bigger than any recipe."

ROASTED
BEET
&
CARROT
CIABATTA

SERVES 8 TO 12

THIS SPECTACULAR RECIPE FROM VALERIE CONFECTIONS MAKES A HERO sandwich, although not in the conventional sense. It's heroic in size. You begin with a whole ciabatta, as large as a cutting board, that's split open and slathered with smoky aioli. Then you pile up layers of roasted beets and carrots; feta, pickled onions, and pickled hot peppers; and fistfuls of whole parsley leaves doused with extra-virgin olive oil. What you get is a sandwich that will feed up to a dozen people. It happens to be vegetarian, but nobody will miss the meat. The presentation is impressive enough to be the centerpiece of a buffet, picnic, or party spread.

¾ cup **apple cider vinegar**

1 tablespoon **sugar**

2½ teaspoons **kosher salt,** plus more as needed

1 medium **red onion,** thinly sliced

1 cup **mayonnaise**

1 **garlic clove,** minced

1 teaspoon **Dijon mustard**

1 teaspoon freshly squeezed **lemon juice**

3 tablespoons **harissa paste**

1 teaspoon smoked **paprika**

2 bunches **baby beets,** trimmed

½ cup **extra-virgin olive oil,** plus more for drizzling

Freshly ground **black pepper**

2 bunches small multicolored **carrots,** trimmed and peeled

¼ teaspoon ground **cumin**

1 large (2-foot) **ciabatta**

½ cup crumbled **feta** or **ricotta salata**

½ cup (sliced into rings) **pickled peppers**

2 cups whole fresh **flat-leaf parsley** leaves

1

Preheat the oven to 375°F.

2

Make the pickled onions: In a small bowl, whisk together the vinegar, sugar, and 1 teaspoon of the salt until the sugar dissolves. Add the onion, and toss. Let marinate at room temperature for 1 hour.

3

Make the smoky aioli: In a separate small bowl, whisk together the remaining 1½ teaspoons salt, the mayonnaise, garlic, mustard, lemon juice, harissa, and smoked paprika. Cover the bowl, and refrigerate until ready to use.

4

Combine the beets and ¼ cup of the olive oil in a large bowl, and toss to coat. Season with salt and pepper. Wrap the beets together in aluminum foil, and arrange them in an even layer on a baking sheet. Transfer the beets to the oven and bake until softened, 30 to 40 minutes. Remove from the oven. Let cool for 10 minutes. Peel and cut the beets into ⅓-inch slices.

5

While the beets cook, add the carrots to the same bowl used to coat the beets in olive oil. Add another ¼ cup olive oil and the cumin, and toss to coat. Season with salt and pepper. Arrange the carrots on a separate baking sheet. Transfer to the oven, and bake until the carrots yield to a fork but are still firm at the center, 20 to 25 minutes. Remove the carrots from the oven, and let cool for 10 minutes. Leave the oven on.

6

Slice the ciabatta horizontally. Place the two halves directly on the upper rack of the oven for 1 minute, until warmed but not toasted. Remove from the oven, and place them cut-side up on a flat working surface.

7

To assemble the sandwich, spread smoky aioli over both cut sides of the ciabatta. Arrange the roasted carrots on the bottom half, then layer beets, feta, pickled onion, pickled pepper, and parsley. Drizzle olive oil over the parsley to finish, and press the two halves together. To serve, cut the loaf into 2- or 3-inch slices, securing each with a toothpick.

BROCCOLI IS A VEGETABLE THAT, ALONG WITH BRUSSELS SPROUTS AND KALE, has been reinvented in recent years, thanks to new thinking about old vegetables. Broccoli, in particular, was once thought just to be good for you. In this recipe, which debuted at Ramen Hood cofounder Ilan Hall's previous LA establishment, the Gorbals, the broccoli is just meant to be good. And what could anyone dislike about crispy florets splashed with a spicy vinegar and soy glaze? The first incarnation of this recipe was originally offered as a drinking snack, but at Ramen Hood, it's served more as a side dish to accompany a bowl of noodles. Paired with Ramen Hood's Pressed Cucumber Salad (page 204), it could also be the star of a plant-based dinner. Instead of frying the broccoli, Adele suggests roasting it on a sheet pan in a hot oven.

SOY- CHILE- GLAZED BROCCOLI

½ cup **malt vinegar**

½ cup **soy sauce**

¼ cup **sugar**

½ teaspoon dried **red chile flakes**

2 pounds **broccoli**, cut into florets

Oil, for frying

1 **scallion** (green part only), thinly sliced

1

Combine the vinegar, soy sauce, sugar, and chile flakes in a small saucepan over medium heat. Bring to a boil and cook for 1 minute, then remove the pan from the heat and let cool.

2

Heat 2 inches of oil to 375°F in a deep pot. Working in batches, add the broccoli and fry until lightly browned, about a minute. Drain on a paper-towel-lined tray.

3

In a medium bowl, toss the broccoli with half the dressing, and taste. Add more dressing as you like. Garnish with the scallion and serve with the extra sauce alongside for dipping.

SERVES 8

TORRES PRODUCE OFFERED UP THIS RECIPE WHEN ASKED HOW TO PREPARE chayote, a light-green squash-like vegetable that you see at a lot of Latin greengrocers—and, increasingly, at farmer's markets and in CSA boxes. (If you don't have a chayote on hand, just add some extra squash.) The interesting detail that distinguishes this vegetable soup is how you make the base. First you puree the tomato and aromatics, then you fry the puree in oil to intensify the flavors—a technique used in making many salsas. The result is a bowl of just-cooked vegetables that retain their fresh, distinctive flavors but are knit together by a suave, fragrant, slightly thickened broth.

4 **Roma tomatoes**

½ small **yellow onion,** diced

2 **garlic cloves**

½ teaspoon **kosher salt**, plus more as needed

2 tablespoons **lard** or **vegetable oil**

2 quarts **chicken** or **vegetable stock**

½ pound **carrots**, thinly sliced

2 medium **Mexican squash** or **zucchini**, cut into ½-inch rounds

½ pound small **red potatoes**, thinly sliced

1 large **chayote**, sliced into quarters

4 cups tightly packed **spinach**

1

Place the tomatoes, onion, garlic, and salt in a blender or food processor, and pulse until smooth.

2

Melt the lard in a large pot over medium heat. Add the tomato puree—it will sizzle fiercely—then bring it to a boil, and cook for 5 minutes, or until thickened

slightly. Stir in the stock, and return to a boil. Add the carrots, squash, potatoes, and chayote. Return to a boil again, and cook for 15 minutes, or until the vegetables are tender. Add the spinach, and simmer for 2 minutes longer, just until wilted. Taste and adjust the salt, if needed.

SERVES 8

SOPA DE VERDURA (VEGETABLE SOUP)

★★ BEANS

A POT OF BEANS IS A STAPLE OF HOMEY NOURISHMENT THROUGHOUT THE NEW
World. Case in point is this recipe for stewed pintos from Jose Chiquito. It could hardly be simpler, but the rich, earthy bean taste develops in the pot during its long, slow cooking. When the beans have softened, you flavor the simmering liquids with sautéed aromatics, smoked paprika, and cider vinegar, which sharpens the flavors. The result is beans that taste like beans, their earthiness set off by a highly seasoned broth. Jose Chiquito's beans are also vegetarian and a good example of how much flavor you can create without the addition of meat.

Pinto beans—often paired with rice—are a near-universal partner for tacos, Mexican-style breakfasts, or most other dishes served with salsa and tortillas. Leftover beans can be lightly mashed and reheated ("refried") in a skillet. Some people consider a smear of refried beans an essential addition to a well-dressed *gordita* or *torta*.

2 cups dried **pinto beans** (1 pound), rinsed and drained

2 tablespoons **vegetable oil**

1 medium **white onion**, minced

1 medium **green bell pepper**, seeded and minced

3 **garlic cloves**, minced

1 teaspoon **kosher salt**, plus more as needed

1 teaspoon **sugar**

1 teaspoon **apple cider vinegar**

1 teaspoon **smoked paprika**

1 teaspoon ground **cumin**

1 teaspoon ground **oregano**

1
Place the beans in a medium pot with 4 cups water. Bring to a boil over high heat, then reduce the heat to low. Simmer, partially covered, until the beans are tender, about 2 hours, stirring occasionally.

2
When the beans are nearly done, heat the oil in a large heavy-bottomed sauté pan over medium heat. When the oil shimmers, add the onion, bell pepper, garlic, ½ teaspoon of the salt, the sugar, vinegar, and paprika. Sauté for 2 minutes, or until softened. Add the cumin and oregano, and sauté for 5 minutes longer, stirring constantly. Taste and adjust the seasonings, if needed.

3
Add the aromatic mixture and remaining ½ teaspoon salt to the beans in the pot. Increase the heat to medium-high and bring to a boil. Cook for 20 minutes, until the flavors are melded, stirring frequently to avoid sticking. Taste and adjust the seasonings, if needed.

SERVES 8

SUMMER VEGETABLE Stew WITH GREEN MOLE

PESTO COMPLEMENTS SUMMER VEGETABLES BEAUTIFULLY; SO, TOO, DOES GREEN mole. The idea makes sense: Pesto is a thick sauce of ground pine nuts and herbs. Green mole is a thick sauce of ground pumpkin seeds and herbs. Because green mole is easier to make from scratch that other moles, here's a recipe for how to make it fresh, inspired by Chiles Secos. This stew bears a certain resemblance to succotash, and like succotash—and many stews—its components can vary depending on what you have on hand.

1 teaspoon **kosher salt**, plus more for the pot

½ pound **green beans**, trimmed

½ pound small **potatoes**, mixed purple, yellow, and white

2 ears of **corn**, shucked and de-silked

2 tablespoons **vegetable oil**

1 medium **yellow onion**, cut into ½-inch dice

1 pound **zucchini**, cut into ½-inch slices

2 cups **Green Mole** (recipe opposite)

1 cup **lima beans**, fresh or frozen

1 cup firmly packed sliced **chard** leaves (cut into 1-inch ribbons)

2 tablespoons minced fresh **cilantro**

Juice of ½ **lime**

Fresh **cilantro** sprigs, for garnish

Lime wedges, for garnish

Note: *If you'd rather not make the mole from scratch, green mole paste, which is sold at Chiles Secos and other Latin groceries, provides a shortcut. Melt ⅓ cup mole paste over medium heat and press the paste flat into the pan with a wooden spoon. When it bubbles, whisk in 2 cups water or chicken or vegetable stock, ½ cup at a time, returning the sauce to a boil between each addition. Reduce the heat to low and simmer until the sauce thickens to the consistency of heavy cream, 5 to 10 minutes.*

1
Bring a small pot of well-salted water to a boil over high heat. Add the green beans, and blanch them for 2 to 3 minutes, until tender but still firm. Remove with a slotted spoon, reserving the water in the pot. Return the water to a boil and add the potatoes. Cook until tender, 20 to 25 minutes, depending on their size. Drain the potatoes.

2
Meanwhile, slice the corn kernels off the cob into a large bowl.

3
Heat the oil in a large, heavy-bottomed pot over medium heat. When the oil shimmers, add the onions, season with ⅓ teaspoon of the salt, and sauté for 2 minutes, or until translucent. Add the zucchini, season with another ⅓ teaspoon of the salt, and sauté for 5 minutes, or until the slices start to color.

4
Pour the mole over the zucchini, and bring to a boil. Reduce the heat to low, cover, and simmer for 10 minutes, or until the zucchini just begin to soften. Stir in the lima beans, cover again, and simmer for 5 minutes more, until heated through. Add the chard leaves, and cook for 1 minute, just to wilt them. Add the corn. Cover again, and simmer for 5 minutes more until everything is heated through. Taste, and season with the remaining salt, if necessary.

GREEN MOLE

½ cup **pepitas**

2 tablespoons toasted **sesame seeds**

½ pound **tomatillos**, hulled and quartered

2 cups **chicken** or **vegetable stock**, or **water**

¼ cup chopped fresh **cilantro**

2 cups tightly packed chopped **arugula** or **radish leaves**

2 fresh **serrano chiles,** seeded

½ small **yellow onion**, chopped

2 **garlic cloves**, chopped

1 teaspoon **kosher salt**, plus more as needed

½ teaspoon dried **Mexican oregano**

½ teaspoon **cumin seeds**, toasted and ground

⅛ teaspoon **cayenne** pepper

1 tablespoon **lard** or **vegetable oil**

5

Just before serving, halve the potatoes, and gently fold them into the stew. Garnish with the cilantro, then spritz with lime juice. Serve each portion garnished with an additional whole cilantro sprig and a lime wedge.

SERVES 8

1

Toast the pepitas in a large skillet over high heat for 4 to 6 minutes, taking care not to scorch them. Remove them from the pan to cool.

2

Place the tomatillos and ½ cup of the stock in a blender or food processor and pulse until liquefied. Add the toasted pepitas and sesame seeds, and pulse until smooth. Add the cilantro and arugula, and pulse again until smooth. Add the serrano, onion, garlic, salt, oregano, cumin, and cayenne, and puree. Taste and adjust the seasonings, if needed.

3

Melt the lard in a large skillet over high heat. Pour in the sauce—it will sizzle fiercely. Cook over medium-high heat, stirring frequently, until very thick and nearly dry, 10 to 12 minutes. Whisk in ½ cup of the stock, and return to a boil. Continue to whisk in the remaining stock, in ¼-cup additions, until it is all incorporated. Reduce the heat to low, and simmer for 10 minutes, or until the sauce coats the back of a spoon. Taste and adjust the seasonings, if needed. Store refrigerated in an airtight container for up to 3 days.

MAKES 2 CUPS

ROASTED BUTTERNUT
SQUASH
WITH
DUKKAH

DUKKAH—A CONDIMENT OF NUTS, SEEDS, AND SPICES—HAS ITS ORIGIN IN ancient Egypt, but this innovative recipe from chef Chris Feldmeier redefines dukkah in the modern spirit of vegetable-based cooking. Chris, who ran the kitchen at Bar Moruno, now closed, transforms butternut squash into a spectacular vegetable main dish with heaps of toasty, crunchy spiced nuts. It could even be the centerpiece for Thanksgiving if you celebrate sans turkey.

1 large **butternut squash** (about 2 pounds)

4 tablespoons (½ stick) plus 2 teaspoons **unsalted butter**, softened

¾ teaspoon **kosher salt**

1 teaspoon ground **cumin**

2 teaspoons ground **coriander**

1½ cups unsalted toasted **cashews**, coarsely chopped

⅓ cup toasted **sesame seeds**

1 tablespoon toasted **nigella seeds** (optional)

½ teaspoon **Aleppo chile flakes**, or ¼ teaspoon dried **red chile flakes**

2 teaspoons **vegetable oil**

Honey, for drizzling

1

Preheat the oven to 350°F.

2

Halve the butternut squash lengthwise, and deeply score the flesh with a knife. Rub each half all over with 1 tablespoon of butter per half, and salt generously, using about ¼ teaspoon of kosher salt per half. Arrange the squash on a baking sheet, cut-side up. Transfer it to the oven and roast until just cooked through, about 30 minutes. It should yield slightly when pressed with a wooden spoon. Set aside to cool.

3

While the squash cooks, make the dukkah: Melt 2 tablespoons of butter in a large sauté pan and cook until it begins to brown, about 2 minutes. Add the cumin and coriander, and toast for 2 minutes, stirring to prevent scorching. Add the cashews and toast for 2 minutes, continuing to stir. Add the sesame seeds, nigella seeds (if using), chile flakes, and the remaining ¼ teaspoon salt. Remove the pan from the heat, and set aside.

4

To assemble, heat 1 teaspoon of the oil in a large skillet over medium heat. When it shimmers, add half a roasted squash, cut-side down, and cook until caramelized, 4 to 6 minutes. Transfer to a serving platter, and rub the cut side with a teaspoon of butter. Repeat with the other half. Drizzle with honey, and heap the dukkah on top. Serve hot or at room temperature.

SERVES 6 TO 8 AS A SIDE

SWEETS

MINI CHOCOLATE CHIP COOKIES

SALTED CARAMEL BREAD PUDDING

BANANA PUDDING

CINNAMON ICE CREAM

CHOCOLATE PHOSPHATE

SIZE MATTERS FOR THESE MINI COOKIES FROM VALERIE CONFECTIONS—THEY shouldn't be any larger than a silver dollar, which is just the right size for a guilt-free treat that still gives you a satisfying crunch of buttery cookie, melted bittersweet chocolate, and mineral-y flake salt. For the first months after Valerie and her partner Stan Weightman opened the DTLA branch of their esteemed bakery in mid-2013, Valerie handed out the cookies as a treat after lunch at her long red counter. Since then, business has boomed, and the long red counter has been upgraded with burnished wood. But the cookies are still a staple on Valerie's menu. The only difference is that now, given the demand, she sells them for a dollar—silver or otherwise.

2 cups **all-purpose flour**

1 teaspoon **kosher salt**

1 teaspoon **baking soda**

1 cup plus 2 tablespoons (2¼ sticks) **unsalted butter**, softened

⅔ cup **granulated sugar**

1 cup packed **light brown sugar**

2 large **eggs**

1 teaspoon **vanilla extract**

3 cups coarsely chopped **bittersweet chocolate** (1 pound)

1 tablespoon **fleur de sel** or other flake salt

1

Preheat the oven to 325°F with a rack in the center position. Line a baking sheet with parchment paper. In a medium bowl, sift together the flour, kosher salt, and baking soda.

2

In a stand mixer, beat together the butter, granulated sugar, and brown sugar on medium speed until light and fluffy. Add the eggs and vanilla, and beat until incorporated. Add the dry ingredients, ¼ cup at a time, beating until smooth between each addition. Add the chocolate, 1 cup at a time, and beat until the dough appears evenly speckled. Cover the bowl and place in the refrigerator for 10 minutes to chill the dough for easier shaping.

3

Using a melon baller or a small spoon as a guide, roll a teaspoon at a time of the dough into ½-inch balls. Arrange them on the prepared baking sheet, spaced 2 inches apart. Transfer to the oven and bake for 10 minutes, until lightly colored.

4

Remove the cookies from the oven, and sprinkle a few grains of fleur de sel over each one. Return the cookies to the oven, and bake for 5 minutes more, until golden brown. Transfer the cookies to a rack to cool. Store in an airtight container for up to 3 days.

MAKES 7 DOZEN 1½-INCH COOKIES

MINI CHOCOLATE CHIP COOKIES

SALTED
CARAMEL
bread
PUDDING

VALERIE CONFECTIONS BAKERY & CAFÉ AT GRAND CENTRAL MARKET IS THE second location from partners (in business and life) Valerie Gordon and Stan Weightman Jr. Their original location showcases Valerie's exquisite caramels, chocolates, and petits fours. Valerie's vision for GCM ran toward less precious desserts: things you could easily share or even eat with a plastic spoon as you walked around the Market. Her new line included homey custards, pies, cookies, and this Salted Caramel Bread Pudding. It uses brioche, which is soaked in a lightly sweet vanilla-cream custard and baked until it puffs "with a golden crown," as she says. The salted caramel sauce is a little tricky to make—you have to tend two pots at once and bring them together at the right moment—but it's so good you'll want to eat it with a spoon. Almost since day one, Salted Caramel Bread Pudding was an instant GCM classic. It combines Valerie's instinctive refinement with a simple deliciousness you don't have to think about to enjoy.

6 large **eggs**, beaten

2¾ cups **sugar**

3 cups plus 2 tablespoons **heavy cream**

1 cup **whole milk**

2 teaspoons **vanilla extract**

¼ cup plus 2 tablespoons **light corn syrup**

6 tablespoons (¾ stick) **unsalted butter**, chilled, plus more for greasing

1 teaspoon **fleur de sel** or other flake salt, plus more for sprinkling

2 loaves **brioche** (3 pounds total), crusts removed, cut into 1-inch cubes

Whipped cream, for serving

1

Preheat the oven to 350°F. Make an ice bath by placing a medium bowl into a larger bowl that has been partially filled with ice and water. Lightly grease a 9 × 13-inch baking dish.

2

In a separate medium bowl, whisk together the eggs and ¾ cup of the sugar. Place the bowl in the ice bath to chill. In a medium saucepan over medium heat, combine 2 cups of the cream, the milk, and the vanilla, and bring to a boil. Remove the pan from the heat, and transfer the cream to a heatproof pitcher. Slowly stream it into the egg-sugar mixture in the ice bath, whisking constantly, to form a smooth custard. Cover and refrigerate until ready to use.

3

Make the caramel: Combine the remaining 1 cup plus 2 tablespoons cream and the corn syrup in a small saucepan over low heat. As the cream heats, place the remaining 2 cups sugar in a medium saucepan over medium heat. Using a heatproof spatula, push the sugar to one side of the saucepan. As the sugar begins to melt at the edge, use the spatula to incorporate more sugar, bit by bit, into the liquid caramel.

4

When nearly all the sugar has melted, turn your attention back to the saucepan with the cream. Increase the heat under the cream to medium and bring it to a boil, then remove the pan from the heat and cover it to keep it warm. Continue cooking the liquid caramel until it reaches an amber color, about 10 minutes, then remove that pan from the heat, too.

5

Stream the cream into the caramel—it will bubble up aggressively. When it subsides, stir in the butter, 1 tablespoon at a time. Incorporate the fleur de sel. Cover and set it aside at room temperature.

6

Place the brioche in an extra-large bowl. Pour the custard over it, and using your hands, press and squeeze the brioche cubes until they are evenly saturated. Transfer the brioche to the baking dish. Cover with the caramel sauce, and top with a sprinkle of fleur de sel. Transfer to the oven and bake for 30 minutes, or until the bread pudding puffs like a soufflé with a golden crown. Let cool for 10 minutes before serving with whipped cream.

SERVES 6

BANANA PUDDING

FANS OF BARBECUE JOINTS AND OTHER CASUAL SOUTHERN EATERIES SUCH AS the meat-and-three will tell you that a lunch spot without banana pudding has missed what's good about Southern desserts—they are sweet, nostalgic, and easy to eat. This version of banana pudding from Horse Thief BBQ sticks with tradition, or at least takes a stand on its version of tradition. First, Horse Thief uses cornstarch instead of flour as the thickener—the taste is cleaner. Next, the assembled pudding is topped with whipped cream instead of baked meringue. Are there other ways to do it? Sure. But a glance at the trays passing through Horse Thief's service window on a busy Saturday afternoon shows that GCM visitors have no complaints about this banana pudding. Almost everyone—or at least every group—orders one. In the home kitchen, few other desserts deliver as much pleasure for as little effort.

4½ cups **whole milk**

½ cup **cornstarch**

1 cup granulated **sugar**

½ teaspoon **kosher salt**

4 large **egg yolks**, beaten

3 tablespoons **unsalted butter**, melted

½ teaspoon **vanilla extract**

1 11-ounce box **vanilla wafers**, preferably Nilla Wafers

2 ripe **bananas**, thinly sliced

2 cups **heavy cream**

2 teaspoons **confectioners' sugar**

Note: *There are multiple brands of vanilla wafers, and some overeager dessert masters might even consider making their own "artisanal" version at home. But in barbeque country and throughout the South, the box people reach for when they want to make banana pudding is marked Nilla. 'Nuff said.*

1

In a small bowl, stir together ½ cup of the milk with the cornstarch to make a slurry. Combine the remaining milk with the granulated sugar and salt in a medium saucepan. Warm over medium heat, stirring until the sugar dissolves. Add the cornstarch slurry and continue cooking until the mixture reaches the consistency of condensed milk, about 5 minutes. Remove the pan from the heat.

2

Temper the egg yolks in a medium bowl by dribbling in ¼ cup of the warm custard base while whisking. Stream in the remaining custard base. Whisk in the melted butter and vanilla. Pour the custard back into the saucepan and place over medium heat, stirring until it thickens, 3 to 5 minutes. Remove the pan from the heat.

3

Assemble the pudding: Cover the bottom of a 9 × 9-inch baking pan with vanilla wafers, overlapping them as needed. Add half the pudding, spreading it out to cover. Arrange another layer of vanilla wafers, then a layer of banana slices. Finish with a final layer of pudding. Press plastic wrap directly onto the surface of the pudding to prevent a skin from forming, and refrigerate until chilled, at least 1 hour.

4

Using a whisk or an electric mixer, whip together the cream and confectioners' sugar in a medium bowl until stiff peaks form. Spread it over the pudding in a thick layer and serve.

SERVES 6 TO 8

CINNAMON
ICE CREAM
WITH CANDIED PEPITAS

PERHAPS MORE THAN ANY OTHER VENDOR AT GRAND CENTRAL MARKET, mcconnell's Fine Ice Creams has a universal clientele. A glance at the long line reveals a cross section of seemingly the entire Los Angeles population—every color, creed, age, socioeconomic status, and identity. It makes sense. Because who doesn't crave a scoop of ice cream when the weather turns hot? McConnell's is a through-and-through California brand (see page 234) and this sundae from chef and co-owner Eva Ein with help from pastry chef Jordan Thomas is a perfect example of California's happy mishmash approach to multicultural eating. Its foundation is a rich, custard-based, homemade cinnamon ice cream. Pepitas are the candy-crunch topping, and the finish is whipped cream and salted caramel sauce. Eva suggests serving it with churros alongside, but even without the crispy fried pastry, this fits the bill as a Mexi-Cali ice cream. If such a thing didn't exist before, it does now.

2 cups **heavy cream**

1 cup **whole milk**

⅔ cup **sugar**

⅛ teaspoon **kosher salt**

2 **cinnamon sticks**

1 **vanilla bean**, split and scraped

2 teaspoons **ground cinnamon**

6 large **egg yolks**

Whipped cream, store-bought **salted caramel sauce**, and **Candied Pepitas** (recipe follows), for serving

1

Make an ice bath by placing a medium bowl into a larger bowl that has been partially filled with ice and water. Place 1 cup of cream in the medium bowl.

2

In a medium saucepan over low heat, warm the remaining 1 cup cream, the milk, sugar, salt, and cinnamon sticks, stirring, until the sugar has dissolved, 3 to 5 minutes. Add the vanilla and ground cinnamon, and cook for 1 minute more. Remove the pan from the heat and cover it. Let the custard base steep at room temperature for 45 minutes. Discard the vanilla bean and cinnamon sticks.

3

Whisk the egg yolks in a medium bowl. Slowly stream them into the custard base, whisking constantly. Return the mixture to the saucepan. Cook over low heat, stirring constantly, until the custard coats the back of the spoon, 5 to 7 minutes, or reaches 170°F on a candy thermometer. Do not let custard reach the scalded stage (180°F). Remove the pan from the heat. Strain the custard through a fine-mesh sieve into the bowl with the chilled cream. Stir the mixture over the ice bath until completely cooled. Transfer to an airtight container, and refrigerate for at least 4 hours.

4

Churn the chilled custard in an ice cream maker according to the manufacturer's directions. To serve, scoop the ice cream into bowls. Top with the whipped cream and a drizzle of caramel sauce, and sprinkle the candied pepitas over the top.

SERVES 4 TO 6

CANDIED PEPITAS

MAKES ABOUT 2 CUPS

1½ cups raw hulled **pepitas**

¾ cup **sugar**

1 teaspoon **kosher salt**

2 large **egg whites**, lightly beaten

1

Preheat the oven to 350°F. Line a baking sheet with parchment paper.

2

Combine the pepitas, sugar, salt, and egg whites in a large bowl. Stir to coat the pepitas thoroughly. Pour the mixture onto the prepared baking sheet and, using a spatula, spread it into thin layer. Transfer the sheet to the oven and bake for 30 to 35 minutes, until the pepitas are golden brown. Remove from the oven and cool for 15 minutes.

3

Peel the pepitas off the parchment paper and break them into pieces. Store in an airtight container at room temperature for up to 3 days, or 1 week in the fridge.

MCCONNELL'S CO-OWNER Michael Palmer is a man of many words. Before Michael and his wife, restaurateur Eva Ein, bought McConnell's in 2012, he had a successful career as an advertising executive. Michael can talk at length about what he did for clients—helping them discover their "brand identity" and create a "brand narrative"—and he's good at spinning a personal yarn that weaves together the story, backstory, and back-backstory. Like how it was that he and Eva came to buy McConnell's.

McConnell's Fine Ice Creams was founded in 1949 by Gordon "Mac" McConnell and his wife, Ernesteen. They had moved to Santa Barbara in the 1930s, and he owned some of the country's first health-food stores. One night over a bowl of homemade vanilla ice cream, Mac decided to make ice cream because he was dismayed by what Michael calls the "industrial food complex." In other words, Mac couldn't abide the thought of commercial ice cream made with shortcuts such as artificial flavorings, colorings, and sweeteners. Mac and Ernesteen started selling ice cream made from scratch, with an emphasis on whole, natural ingredients from California's Central Coast—especially local milk and cream from family-owned dairies. McConnell's Fine Ice Creams took off.

Mac died in 1962 and Ernesteen sold the company to Santa Barbaran Jim McCoy, who made a consequential decision that still underpins the quality of McConnell's ice cream. Jim McCoy bought the Old Dairy, which had been supplying milk to McConnell's, making it one of only a half dozen ice cream makers in America—of any size—to operate its own creamery. Most places buy a generic "base" from a manufacturer, mix in flavorings, and slap their own label on the carton. Not McConnell's. Does this udder-to-cone perfectionism matter? *Time* magazine called McConnell's "the best in the world," and the *Wall Street Journal* referred to it as "the frozen gold standard." So maybe.

Which is all a roundabout way of explaining why Michael and Eva bought McConnell's in 2012. A wildfire had just destroyed their home and Michael's newly built winery. He wanted out of advertising and into something with more integrity. Eva had a vision for new California-inspired flavors, such as roasted almond and olive oil. So they took the leap and became the third owners of McConnell's in its seventy-plus year history. The brand's luster had faded a bit since the glory days, but Michael and Eva believed it still had an authentic story to tell about California quality.

That's the long version of the story. In the short version, Michael just says: "I grew up eating McConnell's, and always thought it was something special."

In the summer of 2014 McConnell's opened at Grand Central Market, the company's first Los Angeles–area scoop shop in over thirty years. Eva and Michael continue to live in Santa Barbara, but they pop into the Market frequently to keep the stall shipshape and to oversee their two other newest locations in Los Angeles.

WEXLER'S CHOCOLATE PHOSPHATE IS A CHOCOLATE EGG CREAM BY ANOTHER
name. It's a medium-sweet chocolate soda with a foamy head, a pronounced cocoa flavor, and an appealingly dry edge you can't quite describe. The old-fashioned egg cream/ chocolate phosphate was popularized in New York in the 1920s and associated at the time with Eastern European Jewish immigrants—the same communities that helped define the quintessential New York Jewish delis that inspired Wexler's. An egg cream has neither eggs nor cream, which might be why Micah Wexler calls it by the alternate name to avoid endless explanations. Its fizz and "prickly" sensation come from seltzer water, and the acid phosphate adds the dry tang.

2 cups **filtered water**

1 cup plus 1 tablespoon **sugar**

½ cup **unsweetened cocoa powder**

1½ teaspoons **vanilla extract**

Seltzer water

Acid phosphate

Note: Acid phosphate sounds menacing, but it's a food-safe solution made from dissolved mineral salts. The acidity level is about the same as freshly squeezed lime juice. It is bottled for home use by the Extinct Chemical Company and can be found at high-end liquor stores for cocktail geeks—those places that stock a dozen different bitters—or online.

1

Combine the water and sugar in a small saucepan over high heat. Bring to a boil and cook for 5 minutes. Whisk in the cocoa powder and vanilla, and cook for 1 minute more. Remove the pan from the heat, and let it cool to room temperature.

2

To assemble each serving, combine ¼ cup of the chocolate syrup and 6 drops of acid phosphate in a 16-ounce glass. Add seltzer water to the top, and stir lightly just to combine. Repeat with the remaining ingredients for each serving.

SERVES 10

CHOCOLATE PHOSPHATE

A TYPICAL SUNDAE IS RICH AND DOUBLY SWEET—ICE CREAM TOPPED WITH chocolate and/or caramel syrup, whipped cream, and whatever else you like. This recipe, developed by McConnell's co-owner and chef Eva Ein and pastry chef Jordan Thomas, is also a sundae of sorts, but one that's all about the electric flavors of tropical fruit, citrus, chile, and salt. It begins with homemade mango sorbet, which condenses the flowery, lemony, faintly resinous fragrance and sweet-tart flavor. Fresh pineapple chunks are cooked down with lime juice—no added sugar!—until the natural liquids thicken into sauce, then you stir in more lime juice and zest. The inspired final touch is a sprinkle of chile-lime salt, a mixture eaten on fresh mango in Latin America and other tropical regions around the world. The combination of it all is spicy and titillating, or as Eva says, "ha-cha-cha!"

2½ pounds ripe **mango**, peeled, pitted, and chopped into chunks

⅔ cup **sugar**

1 to 2 tablespoons freshly squeezed **lemon juice**

1 medium **pineapple**, peeled, cored, and diced

4 teaspoons freshly squeezed **lime juice**

3 teaspoons **lime zest**

1 tablespoon **Maldon** or other **flake salt**

1 tablespoon **ancho chile powder**

Lime wedges, for serving

1

In a blender or food processor, combine the mango, sugar, 1 tablespoon of lemon juice, and ⅔ cup water. Pulse until smooth. Taste, and add more lemon juice, if needed. Transfer the mixture to an airtight container and place in the refrigerator to chill for at least 4 hours.

2

Place the pineapple and 2 teaspoons of the lime juice in a small saucepan over medium heat. Bring to a boil, then reduce the heat to low and simmer for 15 to 20 minutes, stirring occasionally, until the liquid has reduced to a syrup. Remove the pan from the heat. Stir in the remaining 2 teaspoons lime juice and 2 teaspoons of the lime zest. Transfer to an airtight container and refrigerate until ready to use.

3

Combine the salt, chile powder, and remaining 1 teaspoon lime zest in a small bowl.

4

Churn the chilled puree in an ice cream maker according to the manufacturer's directions. To serve, scoop the sorbet into a bowls. Top with the pineapple sauce, and sprinkle several pinches of the chile-lime salt over each serving. Garnish with lime wedges.

SERVES 8

MANGO sorbet
WITH PINEAPPLE SAUCE
& CHILE-LIME SALT

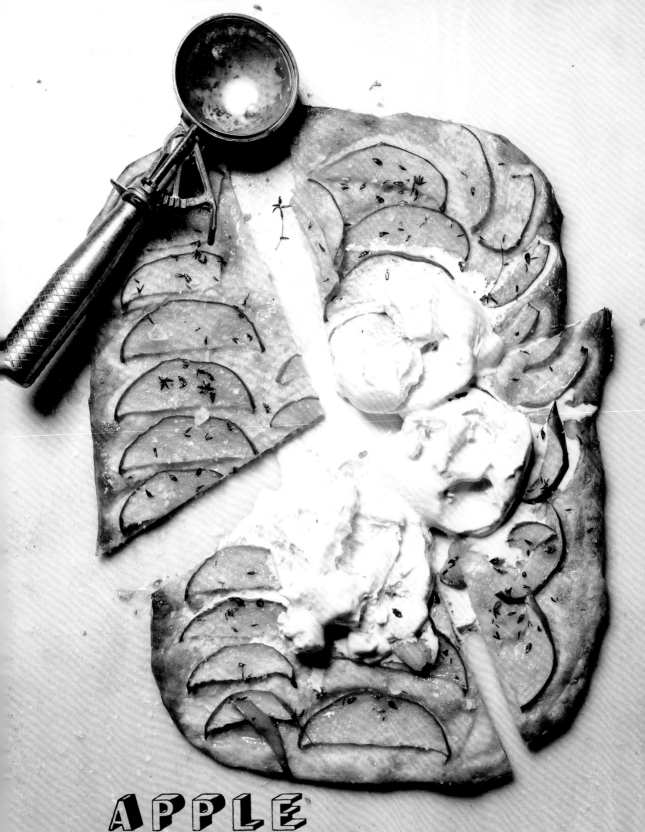

APPLE FOCACCIA

OLIO WOOD-FIRED PIZZERIA

STALL

B-6

OLIO'S CHEF-OWNER BRAD KENT DOESN'T LIKE TO CALL THIS RECIPE A "DESSERT pizza," but that's essentially what it is. You cover stretched pizza dough with sliced apples, fresh thyme leaves, and raw sugar, bake it in a superhot oven, and serve it with vanilla ice cream drizzled with fruity extra-virgin olive oil and sprinkled with a few grains of flake salt. Any leftovers—not that there will be any—could give new meaning to the idea of cold pizza for breakfast. This basic recipe can be adapted by swapping the apples for another fresh fruit in season: peaches or plums, for instance. Or try pressing whole red grapes into the soft dough and sprinkling chopped fresh rosemary and crushed Demerara sugar cubes.

By the way, Italian bakers make a distinction between pizza dough and focaccia dough, but it's a minor, technical one. (Focaccia usually includes more leavening.) A more useful difference is that focaccia is usually shaped into a square or rectangle.

1 **Gala apple**, cored and thinly sliced

½ teaspoon fresh **thyme** leaves

1½ tablespoons **extra-virgin olive oil**, plus more as needed

8 ounces store-bought **pizza dough**, or ½ recipe homemade (page 136)

1 teaspoon **turbinado sugar**

Maldon sea salt or other flake salt

Vanilla ice cream, for serving

1

Preheat the broiler.

2

Arrange the apple slices on a baking sheet in a single layer. Scatter the thyme leaves over the top. Drizzle with the olive oil. Transfer to the oven and broil for 6 minutes, or until the apples are slightly charred and softened. Remove the baking sheet and set it aside to cool. Set the oven to 500°F.

3

Place the pizza dough on a lightly oiled baking sheet. Drizzle the dough and coat your hands with oil, and pull and stretch the dough into a 14 × 10-inch rectangle. Brush the top with more olive oil, and sprinkle generously with turbinado sugar. Arrange the baked apples over the dough.

4

Transfer the baking sheet to the oven, and bake until the crust browns, 5 to 7 minutes. Cut the focaccia into quarters. Serve with vanilla ice cream. Drizzle the ice cream with oil and sprinkle sea salt over the top.

SERVES 4

HORCHATA IS A CHILLED, SWEETENED, MILKY MEXICAN BEVERAGE MADE FROM rice and flavored with almonds and cinnamon. It is essentially a lighter and more economical version of almond milk. At GCM and across Los Angeles, horchata is a favorite drink in hot weather and alongside a plate of tacos—it helps douse the heat in both senses. The rice adds a starchy or chalky quality, and perhaps to compensate, most taquerias use a very heavy hand with the sugar. But the rice flavor is also part of horchata's charm, and this version inspired by GCM vendors reduces the sweetness—a bit. Like sweet tea in the South, horchata's sugary taste and rich mouthfeel make the drink what it is. Of course, those who prefer unsweetened tea might disagree, and by the same token you can adjust the recipe below to suit your own preference.

horchata

¾ cup **long-grain rice**, rinsed and drained

1¼ cups blanched **almonds**

1 **cinnamon stick**, broken into several pieces

⅓ cup **agave syrup**, or more as needed

1 cup **seltzer water**

Ground cinnamon, for garnish

Notes: *Making horchata without a blender or food processor requires too much work to even contemplate.*

The rice and almonds require an overnight soak.

1

In a blender or food processor, combine the rice with 3 cups hot water. Pulse until the rice is broken to bits, about 30 seconds. Transfer to a large jar or bowl, and add the almonds and cinnamon stick. Cover and set aside at room temperature to soak overnight, at least 12 hours and up to 24 hours.

2

Transfer the rice, almonds, cinnamon stick, and soaking water to a blender or food processor. Pulse until smooth, 2 to 3 minutes. Strain the puree through a damp jelly bag or a double thickness of cheesecloth that has been wetted and wrung out over a large bowl. Squeeze to extract as much liquid as possible. Discard the solids.

3

Add 1 cup water to thin the mixture, and stir in the agave. Taste and adjust the sweetness as needed. Transfer to a large pitcher or jar and place it in the refrigerator to chill for 1 hour. To serve, stir in the seltzer. Serve in tall glasses over ice, garnishing each with a pinch of ground cinnamon.

SERVES 4

COCONUT-LIME

COCADAS
(MACAROONS)

LA HUERTA'S STACKED DISPLAY CASES ARE FILLED WITH MEXICAN SWEETS, BUT none of them has the same crossover appeal as the pyramid-shaped, shredded-coconut candies called *cocadas*. That's because they're more or less the same as American-style coconut macaroons (not to be confused with the French *macaron*, a meringue-based cookie). Mexico supplies endless variations of cocada, some made with caramel or dulce de leche and others with condensed milk. This is the latter type, and it literally could not be easier to make: Stir a few ingredients together, shape the mixture into pyramids (or balls or any other shape you like), and bake. The grated lime zest adds perfume and, well, zest to the sweetened coconut, and the sprinkling of sesame seeds on top turn toasty in the oven. The consistency is moist, dense, and chewy; the texture of grated coconut is strangely pleasing. Cocadas keep well, so you can make them in advance for a party or holiday gifting, and they pair well with the sorts of fruit-based candies sold at La Huerta, including *camote* (crystallized sweet potato) and *ate de guayaba* (guava paste).

1 14-ounce bag **sweetened coconut flakes**

¾ cup sweetened **condensed milk**

2 tablespoons **lime zest**

¼ teaspoon **kosher salt**

2 large **egg whites**

1 tablespoon **sesame seeds**

1

Preheat the oven to 325°F. Line a baking sheet with parchment paper.

2

Place the coconut, condensed milk, lime zest, and salt in a large bowl. Stir to combine. Using a whisk or electric mixer, beat the egg whites in a medium bowl to stiff peaks. Gently fold the egg whites into the coconut mixture.

3

To form the macaroons, loosely shape 3 tablespoons of the mixture into pyramids or shaggy balls and place them on the prepared baking sheet, spaced 1 inch apart. Sprinkle about ⅛ teaspoon of the sesame seeds over each one. Transfer the baking sheet to the oven and bake for 20 to 25 minutes, until golden brown with darker tips. Remove from the oven and let cool completely before peeling them off the parchment. Store in an airtight container at room temperature for up to 3 days.

MAKES 18 COOKIES

OLD joe CAKE

SERVES 8

IN 1963, ADELE (PICTURED OPPOSITE) WAS IN PREP SCHOOL IN UPSTATE NEW York with a girl from Virginia. The girl's family sent her the most delicious chocolate cake from home, and she shared it with Adele. Adele asked what it was, and the girl said it was Old Joe Cake. Old Joe, it turned out, was a family servant. This is his recipe.

Does Old Joe Cake have anything to do with Grand Central Market? Not exactly, but it's been a part of Yellin family tradition since Ira and Adele married. Adele was making Old Joe Cake when her two children, Seth and Jessica, were young, and she was making it when Ira bought the Market in 1984. Adele has continued to make the cake since Ira died in 2002, and she's still making it today, fifty-four years since Old Joe sent her the recipe. Why? "Because it's utterly delicious!" she says (which is true). But also because it's a recipe with stories attached.

Surely Old Joe is gone by now. But this recipe—his recipe—shows what happens to the best recipes: They connect us as families, as friends, and as communities.

½ cup (1 stick) plus 1 tablespoon **unsalted butter**, plus more for greasing

2 cups **all-purpose flour**, plus more for the pan

2¼ cups packed **light brown sugar**

5 1-ounce squares **unsweetened chocolate**

½ cup **buttermilk**

1½ teaspoons **baking soda**

1 tablespoon plus 1 teaspoon **vanilla extract**

2 large **eggs**, separated

1 cup **granulated sugar**

¼ cup **cornstarch**

½ teaspoon **kosher salt**

1

Preheat the oven to 350°F. Grease and flour a 9 × 13-inch pan.

2

Sift together the brown sugar and flour into a large bowl. Melt together 3 squares of chocolate, 1 cup water, and ½ cup of the butter in a double boiler. Stir together the buttermilk, baking soda, and 1 tablespoon of the vanilla in a small bowl. Beat the egg yolks lightly in a small bowl. Using a whisk or electric mixer, beat the whites in a medium bowl to stiff peaks.

3

Add the melted chocolate mixture to the dry ingredients, and stir well to combine. Add the egg yolks and stir. Add the buttermilk mixture and stir. Fold in the egg whites. Pour the batter into the prepared pan, transfer it to the oven, and bake for 35 to 45 minutes, until a tester inserted into the middle comes out clean.

4

Meanwhile, make the frosting: Combine the granulated sugar, cornstarch, salt, 1 cup hot water, the remaining 1 tablespoon butter, the 2 squares chocolate, and the teaspoon of vanilla in a medium saucepan over low heat. Bring to a boil, stirring constantly, and continue cooking until the mixture gets thick, 1 to 2 minutes. Remove the pan from the heat. Whisk or beat with an electric mixer until smooth. Return the pan to the heat and continue cooking until thick and bubbling, 3 to 5 minutes more. Remove the pan from the heat, and refrigerate the frosting until the cake is baked and cooled.

5

Frost the cake in the pan. Slice and serve.

ANA MARIA
Horchata 240

BELCAMPO
Banh Mi Lamb Burgers 173

Velvet Steak with
Chimichurri 194

BENTO YA
Curry Udon 122

Tokyo-Style Karaage Fried
Chicken 181

BERLIN CURRYWURST
Sauerkraut Salad 212

CHILES SECOS
Duck Flautas with Dates
& Mole Ajonjoli 100

Linguine with Lamb Sausage
& Mole 127

CHINA CAFE
Chicken Chop Suey 58

Vegetable Chow Mein 119

Seafood Fried Rice 132

CLARK STREET BREAD
Pan Dulce 46

Meyer Lemon Bostock 47

COURAGE & CRAFT
Three Cocktail "Families"
160

DISTRICT MARKET
Ancient Grains Bowl 134

Drought Salad 208

DTLA CHEESE & KITCHEN
Cheesy Potatoes 149

Cheese Platter 152

EGGSLUT
The Slut (Coddled Eggs
with Potato Puree) 43

G&B COFFEE
Yeasted Waffles 63

Tumi (Turmeric Almond-
Macadamia Milk) 65

GOLDEN ROAD BREWING
Vegan Crunchy Avocado
Tacos 106

Artichoke Hot "Wings" 155

HORSE THIEF
Nashville-Style Hot Fried
Chicken Sando 178

Pork Belly 196

Banana Pudding 231

JOSE CHIQUITO
Breakfast Burrito 50

Huevos Rancheros 52

Red Pepper Rice 131

Pinto Beans 219

KNEAD & CO
Spaghetti with Sunday
Gravy 128

Giardiniere 146

Big Meatballs with
Amatriciana Sauce 186

LA HUERTA
Coconut-Lime Cocadas
(Macaroons) 243

LA TOSTADERÍA
Tostada Mixta 96

Avo Puree 85

MADCAPRA
Herb-Tahini Dip 144

Spiked Beet-Sumac Soda 169

Tomato Salad with Chile,
Black Pepper & Cardamom
203

A **TOMAS MARTINEZ** Tacos Tumbras a Tomas & Ana Maria / B **REED HERRICK** DTLA Cheese & Kitchen / C **VALERIE GORDON** Valerie Confections Bakery & Cafe / D **MICAH WEXLER** Wexler's Deli / E **MANUEL MARTINEZ** Ana Maria & Tacos Tumbras a Tomas / F **MICHAEL PALMER & EVA EIN** McConnell's Fine Ice Creams / G **MARLON MEDINA** Jose Chiquito / H **LYDIA CLARK** DTLA Cheese & Kitchen / I **DAVID TEWASART** Sticky Rice & Sticky Rice II / J **KYLE GLANVILLE** G&B Coffee / K **CHARLES BABINSKI** G&B Coffee / L **ZACK HALL** Clark Street Bread / M **LENA & HARDEEP MANAK** Berlin Currywurst / N **FERNANDO VILLAGOMEZ** Villa Moreliana & La Tostadería / O **RAHUL KHOPKAR** Ramen Hood / P **CHRISTOPHE HAPPILLON** The Oyster Gourmet / Q **BRAD KENT** Olio Wood-Fired Pizzeria / R **RINCO CHEUNG** China Cafe

ACKNOWLEDGMENTS

FROM ADELE:

Three families over these one hundred years have nurtured and reinvented the Market to meet the needs of their respective generations. In creating this book, I wish to honor the Laughlin family, the Lyon family, and Ira Yellin for their commitment to the Market and the city of Los Angeles. They allowed the Market to grow, thrive, and change.

So many people helped Ira during his tenure at Grand Central Market—far too many to name here. What falls to me now is to thank the people who helped me transform the Market on my watch. First, I want to acknowledge the development firm RM|d for their help refocusing our project. Next, Christophe Farber has been our business director extraordinaire. Joseph Shuldiner and Kevin West, partners in Headspace Consulting, brought to us ideas and chefs that matched my vision. Their taste and creativity is evident throughout the space. (Thank you to Kevin a second time for writing this book and to Braden Graeber for helping with the recipes.)

I also want to acknowledge Jim Yeager and Roberta Silverman from breakwhitelight for their astute PR management; my lawyer and friend Richard Moss for his support and advice; the late Ron Rogers; architects Brenda Levin and Andrea Rawlings; and designers Roxanne Danner and Clark Stiles at Ludlow Kingsley.

A special thank-you to the dedicated group who make the Market run every day: Benito Chavez, Gina Mellendrez, Tulia Williams, Todd Videon, and Farshad Moray. Thank you also to Filomena Eriman, Anne Peaks, and Massimo Avincola for their years of work.

My thanks are due to the city of Los Angeles and the City Council for supporting Ira's idea at the beginning, when it seemed like an impossible feat, and for believing in my vision and continuing to support the Market during the past five years. In particular, I want to acknowledge Councilmember José Huizar for his Bringing Back Broadway initiative, and Jessica Wetherington McClain, its executive director. I am also grateful to Mayor Eric Garcetti and the staffs at the MTA and CRA.

Last and certainly not least are my family and closest friends, who have lived with me through the ups and downs of this project. Thanks to my Sunday walking group: Aileen Adams, Kathleen Brown, Diane Cooke, Janet Rappaport, Heidi Schulman, and Diane Wayne. To my family friends Art and Dahlia Bilger, Toni and Bruce Corwin, Nancy Englander and Harold Williams, Liz Familian, Marcia and Paul Herman, Mickey Kantor, Lynn Rosenfeld, and Lisa Specht. To my assistant, Leslie Hopp. And, with special warmth, thank you to my loving and supportive children, Seth Yellin and Jessica Yellin, and my daughter-in-law, Jenny Comita. Everyone has made a significant contribution in his or her own way.

FROM KEVIN:

The biggest debt of gratitude for this book—and for the revitalization of Grand Central Market—goes to the remarkable vendors who give the place its reason to be. They make GCM a gathering place for the cuisines and cultures of Los Angeles, and their recipes made this book possible. Thank you all, each and every one.

Endless thanks to Adele Yellin, the Boss Lady of Grand Central Market. I continue to be amazed that back in 2012 Adele chose me and Joseph Shuldiner to advise her despite our complete lack of relevant credentials. I'm honored to have had the chance to help shape the Market's revitalization and tell its stories. Likewise, special thanks to Adele's daughter-in-law and my old colleague, Jenny Comita. A fortune-teller in Paris once told me that a coworker would someday reappear in my life and unexpectedly change my direction; I never understood until Jenny introduced me to Adele and GCM.

In one sense, this book happened because of Jim Yeager, who caught hold of a fugitive thought and developed the idea of creating a GCM cookbook as part of the centennial anniversary celebration. In the early stages of putting it together, Andrea Alonso's charm and quick thinking gave the project a jump start. In the later stages, Benito Chavez's persistence and steady humor insured that the last threads got tied up. Christophe Farber had a hand—or, rather, a word—in all stages of the book's creation, from the first conversation to the last page proofs. Throughout, I relied on his smarts, sarcasm, pitch-perfect ear, and Solomonic judgment, and I trusted his opinion (on nonculinary matters, at least) more than anyone's, including my own. Thanks, Farber.

Editor Amanda Englander had envisioned what this cookbook could be even before Jim brought the idea to Adele and the GCM team. I am deeply grateful to her for her intuitive grasp of what makes the Market unique and her ability to translate that spirit of community onto the page. I equally doff my hat to the rest of the Clarkson Potter team, especially Stephanie Huntwork, Laura Palese, Ada Yonenaka, Philip Leung, Kathy Brock, and Sara Rennert for their roles in creating a cookbook that looks and feels as vibrant, busy, and alive as the Market itself, and to Natasha Martin and Carolyn Gill for getting it in front of the world.

Photographer Johnny Autry and his assistant, Nick Iway, brought to bear an incredible work ethic and an admirable sense of creative calm under challenging conditions. Their weeklong shoot coincided almost to the hour with the heaviest rainstorms to drench LA in over a decade, yet Johnny's pictures somehow captured the Market precisely as I had come to know it over the four previous years of drought and endless sunshine. Charlotte Autry's food styling in the studio was also masterful, the happy result of abundant talent and a self-effacing ego. She's also the nicest person you'd ever want to meet.

My longtime agent, David Kuhn, and his colleague Kate Mack of Aevitas Creative Management once again showed the keen commitment, insight, and ongoing support that makes a project like this possible. Thank you especially to Kate for her tireless work.

A cookbook usually takes a year, and we had only six months to pull it off. What got squeezed out in the crunch were the rhythms of normal life. Without having asked for it, Braden Graeber bore the brunt and held steady. Thank you, B, thank you, thank you—for putting up with me, for keeping me on the rails, developing and testing recipes, cooking, and all the rest of it. I promise not to put you through this again. Joseph—Headspace has been the most enjoyable collaboration of my career.

And finally, Del and Christine Martin, Marc Gordon and Cheryl Zellman, and Felix and Cara Carroll made a newcomer feel at home in the Berkshires. Thanks to them all.

Grateful acknowledgment is made to *Los Angeles
Times* for permissions to reprint an excerpt of
"27. Grand Central Market" from Jonathan Gold's
101 Best Restaurants by Jonathan Gold, originally
published in *Los Angeles Times* on November 4, 2015.
Copyright © 2017 by *Los Angeles Times*. Used with
permission.

Library of Congress Cataloging-in-Publication Data is
available.

ISBN 978-1-524-75892-9
eBook ISBN 978-1-524-75893-6
Printed in China

Book and cover design by Laura Palese
Front cover oilcloth: www.oilcloth.com

10 9 8 7 6 5 4 3 2 1

First Edition